PROTECT
the
DREAM

Other Works by Kit Cummings

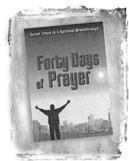

PROTECT
the
DREAM

40 Days of Power

KIT CUMMINGS

Award-Winning Author and International Speaker

Alpharetta, GA

ISBN: 978-1-61005-626-7

Library of Congress Control Number: 2017914503

10 9 8 7 6 5 4 3 2   1 1 1 3 1 7

Printed in the United States of America

This paper meets the requirements of ANSI/NISO Z39.48-1992 (Permanence of Paper)

Foreword

The human brain is malleable. From a young age, we are constantly absorbing information through what we watch, what we listen to, and whom we are surrounded by. All that we know comes from watching others do it first. That's why we so easily become like our parents. We mimic everything from our taste in music to which shoe we put on first, and that is why role models play such a vital role in molding human beings as they grow and mature.

For me, my biggest role model was my dad. As a kid, my dad was how I pictured all adults: strong, supportive, and stern, but happy and playful enough to be my best friend. I grew up playing all kinds of sports, and I was addicted to the competition. I wanted to win. But more than anything, I wanted to impress my dad. When I would lose, I would tear up in frustration because I let him down—my role model. "How will I ever be good enough? My dad didn't lose in the playoffs. He would have made that shot." But the more I beat myself up, the less I cared about becoming my dad.

As I got older, my role models changed. I began seeing faults in my father, and celebrities and pro athletes seemed more like the life I dreamed of living. Michael Vick, LeBron James, and Lil Wayne became my image of the ideal life. I was fascinated by the flashiness: the money, the success, and the fame. So much so that I subconsciously began to surround myself with the wrong crowd. The "cool kids" got all the girls, they had all the parties, and they won all the championships. I wanted to be like them.

It wasn't long before I lost sight of my morals and values. Popularity consumed my inner self, and things that used to terrify me were no longer scary. My role model was now my best friend Troy. Troy was the coolest kid in school, and he wasn't afraid of anything. Which meant, as Troy's best friend, I couldn't be afraid of anything. I got involved in a lifestyle full of danger and excitement, and it was exhilarating. I was finally talking to pretty girls and getting invited to parties. I was finally hearing my name around school and getting the attention I deserved. But it was short lived.

Soon enough, Troy got into some real trouble, and he wasn't around anymore. I would have cared if he was actually my friend, but I saw it as an opportunity to fill the position. "Put me in, coach," I told the universe, and the universe spoke back. I got caught acting foolish, and was involved in a situation that could have ruined my life. I took a hard fall, one that pushed me closer to the edge than ever before. It took time to reevaluate and set my life back on the right path. I had to find new friends and new role models, people who shared my vision and held the same things close to heart. I have come so far, and it's funny. I'm more like my original role model than ever before—my father. Who knew he had it figured out all along?

Today's generation lacks the right role models. We live in a culture fascinated by glitz, glam, and gangsters. It's time for the youth to stand up and become the new generation of role models. Teens could save lives just by living life the right way. Who do you want to be? How are you going to get there? Blaze the path so others can follow in your footsteps. It's time to get to work.

—Cole Cummings

Our first POPP Protect the Dream interns at the University of Georgia

Introduction

Welcome to this forty-day journey to change the way you look at things. As a young athlete, you have been chosen to take part in a special project. Many groups, in various places, have experienced dramatic transformation from embracing the principles of this project. Your individual outcomes are up to you. I invite you to test yourself, and your teammates. Discover what hides deep inside of you, things you have yet to uncover. Dig deep, where purpose, passion, and power reside.

Your generation, "Generation Z," is poised to change the world with your collective voice. You understand the importance of connection more than previous generations have. You care about humanity more than most people think. You care more about this planet than other generations have. You are more innovative and creative, and you do not settle for inactivity or delay. You expect things to happen NOW, much quicker than even Millennials do. You've also managed to create a style of clothing, music, media, movies, games, communication, art, and language that is extraordinarily unique. Don't worry about what older generations are saying about you. Your generation is the most brilliant and aware, and you are on the brink of changing the world forever. We are seeing more and more thirty-something-year-old billionaires emerge, and at a pace no one could have imagined twenty years ago. The reason? Innovation and fresh, new ways of thinking. Can you imagine some of your generation's superstars when they reach the age of forty? However, with great gifts and talents come great responsibility.

You have been chosen for a very important campaign. Whatever the reason you made the cut, you are now responsible for the way you lead. And the stakes couldn't be higher. Violence, overdose, suicide, and accidental death are reaching epidemic levels among your peers. Parents, teachers, law enforcement, preachers, and coaches are at a loss as to how to stop this trend, and how to turn the tide. We are losing a generation of brilliant, strong, and beautiful young people because of foolishness, carelessness, and reckless behavior. When I was in high school and college in the eighties, I never had any friends who overdosed, or died in an accident; went to prison, or took their own life. It rarely if ever happened where I grew up. We didn't have gangs in our communities, and hard drugs were relatively unseen at my high school. We didn't have the technology to cyberbully someone—that could only happen in the halls or on the playground. All that has changed. I would bet that any young person reading this knows someone personally in every one of those categories. This is tragic.

However, there IS a solution, but the answer might not be what you think. The answer is YOU. Principals, teachers, coaches, and parents can only do so much. You have the influence and you have the power, if you choose to exercise it. Your generation is poised to change the world. Your generation is more socially, environmentally, scientifically, politically, and technologically aware than any generation that has preceded you. You have mastered technology and media and have the potential to touch millions with a keystroke. In twenty years, YOU will be leading the world. That can either be a blessing or a curse—it is up to you to determine which it will be.

Kit and original POPP Founders inside a maximum-security prison

This project is about pushing yourself to create big dreams, develop grand visions, and equipping you with the tools to protect those dreams at all costs. But it's not just about protecting your dream; it's also about taking responsibility to protect others' dreams as well. You have the privilege, you have the influence, you have the voice, and now you have the responsibility. **Protect the Dream**. Let's get started.

Letics Soccer Club founder Jeff Wadstrom and head coach Ulises Romero, as we are about to enter a juvenile prison in Tijuana to play an exhibition game for peace. The "Boys of Tijuana" and their work getting kids off the streets and away from the cartels inspired the POPP Protect the Dream Campaign in the US.

The POPP Process

The Power of Peace Project (POPP) was forged inside Georgia's most violent and dangerous maximum-security prison, in the midst of a gang war. It spread through prisons and juvenile detention centers around the country, and even down into Tijuana where we worked with cartel members, tough kids, and recovering addicts. Then it spread to inner-city schools, and now it has branched out to the suburbs. It began when twelve young, diverse rival gang members, doing life sentences, banded together to start a peace movement where few thought it was even possible. Those men changed my life, and the course of my work, forever. That one idea led to an experiment, evolved into a program, and then became a movement. It has taken me to prisons and schools around the world to four different continents. Those original twelve convicts proved to me that if peace can happen there, then it can happen anywhere—even at your school. Why not here, why not now, and why not YOU?

Here's How It Works

Every week we will commit to a new step, break an unhealthy habit, and pick up a new practice. Each day we will study an iconic athlete and learn two new quotes from that champion. We will have a daily action-challenge that all participants will attempt as a team. Journaling in your 40 Days of Power training manual is encouraged. Each week the POPP team will gather for a group meeting and for time with your Power Partner. You will grade yourself on effort, attitude, and intensity. Every player will complete a Champions of Peace paper, and standouts will be featured at the graduation celebration upon the conclusion of our project. You will receive a wristband and a book at the start, and later earn a T-shirt and a certificate of achievement, along with a special banquet, at the 41st Day Celebration.

This program works if you work it. Wear your Protect the Dream wristband at all times to remind you of the commitment you have made to yourself, your coaches, and your teammates. As other students see it and ask what it's all about, be prepared to answer. Don't skip any of the steps, don't attempt to shortcut the process, don't cheat yourself or your teammates, and don't quit. Hold one another accountable, and give it everything you've got. What have you got to lose? Breakthroughs await.

Seven Steps to Power

These are the unhealthy habits that are stealing your power and robbing you of your potential. These habits must be broken, quarantined, deleted, and replaced. We must begin with ACTION not just on the playing field, but on the mental battlefield. We will have victory if we fully commit and trust the process.

Today I pledge to do my very best to live by the following seven principles for the next forty days:

1) I will not complain about anyone or anything; I will remain diligent and determined.
2) I will not blame anyone for my situation; I will actively search for solutions.
3) I will not make excuses for my problems or mistakes; I will take action.
4) I will not be a victim; I will take 100 percent responsibility for my life, no matter who is at fault.
5) I will not prejudge people, situations, or opportunities; I will observe and overcome.
6) When wrong, I will promptly admit it and quickly make amends.
7) I will treat my opponents with dignity and respect, whether we win or lose.

Signature:

School:

Date:

Hillgrove
Hawks

Harrison
Hoyas

Alexander
Cougars

Allatoona
Buccaneers

Fellowship Christian Paladins

Personal Power Goals
SMART Goals are one of the keys to victory:

Specific
Specific goals help us focus our efforts and clearly define what we want to accomplish. "I want to increase my bench press by forty pounds" is better than "I want to get stronger."

Measurable
Your goals must be measurable. In other words, there is usually a number involved—speed, times per week, weight, reps, tackles, victories, etc. When you create a goal that is measurable, it's easy to determine when you're getting closer or if you've reached your goal.

Attainable
Nothing happens without action. Your goal must promote action, and you must be able to break your goals down into actionable tasks. If you can't control the outcome of your goal ("I want to win the lottery"), it's not a real goal. It's a wish and a dream. Your goals must be something you can control.

Realistic
Your goals should inspire you. However, they should be in the realm of possibility. "I want to run a 4.4 in my forty-yard dash." That's a goal, but if your current best is a 4.8, then it isn't necessarily realistic. (This might be an area you want to get advice from your coaches on.)

Time Specific

Anybody who starts a goal with "Someday I want to. . ." will never achieve that goal. It's too vague, and there is no time frame. The best goals have deadlines. The more specific the goal, the better. Choose a definite finish date, and make your goals relevant to what you and your team are trying to achieve this season.

Top-Ten Personal Goals for the Next Forty Days

*(Review these goals **every day** as you begin your daily practice. We recommend that you write the first draft in pencil, as you will be refining them throughout the project.)*

1.

2.

3.

4.

5.

6.

7.

8.

9.

10.

YOU PLAY LIKE YOU PRACTICE. THE SAME IS TRUE IN LIFE.

Participate in our life-changing 40 Days of Power program
and get to work changing some lives of your own.

PowerOfPeaceProject.com

POWER
OF PEACE
P R O J E C T

Choose a Power Partner

Two are better than one. When one falls down, his brother can help him up. Choose wisely—the quality of your Power Partner will greatly affect your chances of success.

Choose Two POPP Captains

Now choose your seven-on-seven teams. Alternate picks like you did back in the day. We will have weekly competitive seven-on-seven exercises.

RPM for POWER

- Ask yourself, "What is it that I want?" Start with your outcome in mind. Get very clear about the RESULT you want at the end of this forty-day campaign. Be specific and focus on it every day. This is your WHAT.

- Now ask yourself WHY you want what you want. This is your PURPOSE for achieving your goals. The bigger your why, the better. If your "why" is not bigger than your largest obstacle, your greatest fear, and your most sophisticated excuse, then you will quit every time. No quitting allowed over the next forty days.

- Finally, ask yourself HOW you will achieve these goals. This is your METHOD. Time to stretch yourself and push yourself above and beyond your current limits. Keep this book with you as you go, and USE it.

- Use the RPM process with your Power Partner, and review and critique one another's goals.

Dream Killers

We will tackle one Dream Killer a week over the next forty days. These are the potential pitfalls that will threaten the big dreams you have for your life, and the dreams of your teammates and classmates. By halftime you will have chosen one of the seven Dream Killers as your platform on which you will build your Power of Peace Project Campaign at your school.

- Week One: Promoting a Bullying Spirit
- Week Two: Irresponsible Social Media
- Week Three: Objectifying Classmates
- Week Four: Unhealthy Relationships
- Week Five: Disrespecting Authorities
- Week Six: Alcohol and Drug Abuse
- Overtime: Lowering Scholastic Standards

HALT

The brain is a learning machine and a storyteller. It was not designed to make you happy, but rather to keep you alive. It is the operating system for your instrument (your physical body). It is always changing, based on the way you think and experience life, and it is the control center and the decision-making apparatus. Every day we are constantly downloading information into our supercomputer. Sometimes we are downloading helpful "apps" that make life easier for us, so we can work efficiently and effectively.

Other times we are unknowingly downloading "viruses," which burn valuable energy and take away our personal power. Apps, or positive tools that you pick up, are energy FILLERS, while viruses are destructive energy DRAINS. Choose wisely what information gets through your Gates: Eye Gate, Ear Gate, and Mouth Gate. Your brain is always paying attention to what you're paying attention to, so learn to control the flow of information into your control center.

YOU are the captain of your ship, and you are responsible for utilizing your brain to its highest potential. Here are the states in which our supercomputer slows down and makes the worst decisions:

- **H**ungry
- **A**ngry
- **L**onely
- **T**ired

Learn to recognize the signs, and when you sense these states, hit the brakes. Do not make big decisions when you are highly emotional. HALT, and take some time to make the best possible choice. This will help you avoid the Dream Killers. They're all around you, but you can learn to navigate the minefield and return to the pathway to your dreams.

"We live in an age fit for heroes. No time has ever offered such perils or prizes. . . . The test of this century will be whether man confuses the growth of wealth and power with the growth of spirit and character."

—Vince Lombardi

In the first half of our Protect the Dream Campaign, we will focus on character. Character is who you are when nobody is watching. It's the REAL you. It's time to get to work on the inner core, and I don't mean weight training. Let's go inside and begin the workout.

Week One

*I will not complain about anyone
or anything; I will remain
diligent and determined.*

Complaining is a weak and impotent strategy for failure. It is a garbage magnet and an unhealthy habit that must be broken. It's like carrying a violin around and looking for people who will listen to your sad song. When we complain, we are setting the stage to avoid personal responsibility, not if, but WHEN we fail. Champions do not complain, they work. Losers unknowingly create an energy of failure by their powerful and creative words. Be mindful of how you finish this short sentence: "I am _____." Why define yourself as tired, sore, weak, or inadequate? Train yourself through powerful "I am" statements to create effective and productive habits in the brain. Here are some that I use on a regular basis: "I always finish strong. I get stronger as the game goes on. I always finish the drill. I deserve the victory. I am a champion. I've made it through tougher times than this. Bring it." Choose power phrases that work for you.

POPP Power Principle #1
We Find What We Believe We Deserve.

Not that we necessarily get what we deserve, but rather, we tend to notice and "find" what we BELIEVE we deserve. The great ones believe they will win, unless they simply run out of time. We all carry mental messages deep in our subconscious. They were planted there as thoughts and ideas that we've run through so many times that eventually we accepted them as reality (but that doesn't mean they are true; they must be challenged). It is said that roughly 95 to 97 percent of the things we will do today are driven by the subconscious. For that reason, we must actively and consciously get involved in the conversation happening in our minds. That mindless chatter, if unattended, can steal your power and shipwreck your goals and dreams. Powerful mantras and self-talk are the way to reprogram your subconscious, which drives your behavior and performance. The greats have mastered their inner dialogue and know how to bring weak thoughts into submission.

CAUTION FLAG

Pay attention to all the violence you witness this week: in your movies, in your music, and on your social media. The first step is awareness—just begin to notice.

Watch Week-One POPP Video

(Short inspirational YouTube clip. These will be chosen each week by a POPP Captain to motivate the team.)

This week we will get into the minds of those who have achieved what few others ever have. This week: **NO COMPLAINING.** Reclaim your power.

Coaches Corner

Vince Lombardi[1]

I never realized how significant the coaches were in my life until I got older and no longer played sports. I later learned that powerful life lessons were secretly imbedded in all those hours of drills, challenges, rebukes, practices, talks, and scrimmages. I had no idea. I wish I had them all recorded so I could go back and listen again, all these years later. What if I had paid closer attention growing up? What if I had truly listened and applied all the different pieces of wisdom, and what seemed to be insignificant pointers, given by these men and women attempting to shape my young life?

Vince Lombardi was a player's coach. His players would literally run through a wall for him. They loved him, respected him, feared him, and were intensely loyal and protective of him—he was like their daddy. Could you treat your coach that way? Could you put aside your preconceived notions and all the things you think you know, and really listen to your coach? I hope so. You'd be amazed at what you could learn. This week I want you to show them respect for their position, for their dedication, and for their sacrifice. They deserve it.

---

[1] Vince Lombardi Biography, "About Vince Lombardi," Family of Vince Lombardi c/o Luminary Group LLC, accessed August 22, 2017, http://www.vincelombardi.com/about.html.

Achievements

When people think of a football coach, they often think of Lombardi. His ability to inspire, motivate, teach, and get the most out of his players was second to none. Coach Lombardi turned the Green Bay Packers into one of the most dominant NFL teams in the sixties. His teams won five NFL Championships, as well as being the victors in Super Bowls I and II. Lombardi died of colon cancer at the age of fifty-seven in 1970. Thousands of fans and mourners packed two separate funerals to honor the beloved coach, and shortly after his death, he was elected into the Pro Football Hall of Fame. The NFL also honored Coach Lombardi by having his name forever adorn the trophy awarded to the Super Bowl Champion each year. How will you show your coaches how much you appreciate their sacrifice, and your gratitude for the way they pour their lives into you?

"I firmly believe that any man's finest hour, the greatest fulfillment of all that he holds dear, is that moment when he has worked his heart out in a good cause and lies exhausted on the field of battle—victorious."

"The real glory is being knocked to your knees and then coming back. That's real glory. That's the essence of it."

—Vince Lombardi

Week-One Local Flavor

Coach David Ironside
Hillgrove Hawks
Powder Springs, GA

"I have been coaching for twenty-five years. Coaching was a natural transition for me after playing in college. We all say we got into coaching to teach boys how to become men through the game we love, which is partially true. Honestly, I loved the game, the companionship of a team, and competing. I strived to teach the right things, values, ethics, and discipline. However, as the years pass you can stray a little and be way off target. This past off-season I was searching for answers. There must be more. It seemed our worth and value as a coach was tied to wins and losses. I talked with other coaches and pastors, and read everything I could get my hands on. What I realized was that I was a very passionate coach who cared deeply about his players, coaches, and winning. After my search for knowledge, I concluded that I must put purpose over passion. My purpose as a coach is to use the talent God has given me to invest in the lives of others for the kingdom. Period. I am to work as hard as I can to prepare, love, and serve coaches and players. I know God placed Kit and the Power of Peace Project in my life at just the right time when my heart was right for this opportunity. It has been just as good for our coaches who were involved as it was for our players."

Coach Jeffrey Wishon

"I have been coaching high school football for the past twelve years as an offensive-line coach. When I was in high school, I had coaches who had a tremendous influence on my life. That is one of the main reasons I became a teacher and a coach. I hoped to be able to have the same impact on high school athletes that these coaches had on my life. I knew the Protect the Dream program would be a great avenue for me to work with our athletes and invest in their lives off the field. Through the POPP program, I have been able to witness a change in the lives of our athletes. They are aware of their actions and the impact they can have on our school. The program has reinforced to me that my role as a coach is much more than just the X's and O's of football. If I can use this platform as an avenue to make our players better students, employees, husbands, and fathers as they grow up, then that will be a much greater accomplishment than anything I could have achieved on a Friday night as a coach. Kit has become a member of the Hillgrove family. After the forty days were finished, he was just getting started. He has been supportive of our kids and coaches from the beginning, and continues to be a mentor to our boys. The effort he has given to this program and the passion he has for serving our team is something I will be forever grateful for!"

"I never smile when I have a bat in my hands. That's when you've got to be serious. When I get out on the field, nothing's a joke to me. I don't feel like I should walk around with a smile on my face."

"My motto was always to keep swinging. Whether I was in a slump or feeling badly or having trouble off the field, the only thing to do was keep swinging."

—Hank Aaron

Day One

From My Perspective

I grew up in Atlanta, so I was able to follow much of the latter part of Hammerin' Hank Aaron's career. My parents were present the night he broke the all-time homerun record at Fulton County Stadium, and I remember watching it at home as a little boy. He chased the most-prized record in all of sports for decades, and he did it when there were many who didn't want him to succeed. However, he was tougher than his opposition, and he outlasted them. Do you have greatness hiding inside of you? If it's going to emerge, you've got to be tougher than the "haters" out there who have no dreams. Outwork them, and prove them wrong. Over the next forty days, we will set our attention and focus on thinking, training, and competing like Champions. Today we begin.

Fascinating Facts

Hank Aaron was a twenty-five-time All Star and held the career-home-run record for an incredible thirty-three years. What many people don't know is that while he was chasing that coveted record, he faced death threats, racist letters, and nasty slurs. He had a bodyguard who traveled with him at games and on the road, simply because he was a person of color. What is the biggest obstacle or threat that you face playing the game you love? Be grateful you can play wherever, whenever, however, and with whomever you choose to play today. And remember that others paved the way for you to have the privileges you have today. Work like you appreciate their sacrifice.

Today's Achievements

Each day, write down your achievements and breakthroughs for the week. Example: "Today I caught myself every time I was making an excuse, and I got back on track quickly." Acknowledge your progress and focus on what you are doing RIGHT, not just your mistakes. You are building momentum, self-esteem, and confidence. Remember, reviewing your goals daily and recording your progress is crucial to establishing new habits, and reaching your goals and dreams.

Today I want you to focus on "just one more." Overcome the tendency to do the minimum, or just whatever is required. In the weight room, do "just one more rep" for your teammates. On the field, do "just one more sprint" for your coaches. At home, do "just one more chore" for your family. Develop the habit of ONE MORE. Go above and beyond expectations.

TODAY'S ACTION-CHALLENGE

"Winners, I am convinced, imagine their dreams first. They want it with all their heart and expect it to come true. There is, I believe, no other way to live."

"Cause there's only one reason for doing anything that you set out to do. If you don't want to be the best, then there's no reason going out and trying to accomplish anything."

—Joe Montana

Day Two

From My Perspective

I was lucky enough to watch Joe Montana's entire career. While not the most physically gifted quarterback, he more than made up for it with his mind, his will, and his heart. He was a true winner, and he played the game with an ever-increasing pursuit of excellence. The teams he captained in the eighties and nineties were pure precision, like a fine-tuned machine. Hours and hours of perfect practice, away from the spotlight, set the stage for thrilling comebacks and two-minute drives. You can be like him, but you can't fake this funk. You've got to put in the work. Don't whine, just grind.

Fascinating Facts

Joe Montana was a three-time Super Bowl MVP and a four-time Super Bowl Champion. He could have chosen to play college basketball, as he was offered a scholarship to play at North Carolina State University, before choosing to go to Notre Dame to play football.[2] Life all comes down to choices. I wonder how many lives that one decision impacted. I bet he would have still been a winner if he had pursued basketball, but sports history would have been

---

[2] Biography.com, s.v. "Joe Montana," last updated February 9, 2016, https://www.biography.com/people/joe-montana-9412332.

forever altered. For Joe, it wasn't as much about athletic ability, but rather attitude, effort, and intensity. Some of you have been gifted with the ability to play more than one sport. Do you honor the gift that your Creator blessed you with? Joe made the most of his—now let's see if you will.

Today's Achievements

Today I want you to observe your mind and eavesdrop on your thoughts. See how many times you can catch yourself complaining in your mind throughout the day. I want you to choose a Power Word you can utilize every time you catch yourself complaining—you must break the habit. An example would be GRATITUDE. Write it down, and say it with feeling and emotion whenever you catch yourself in a negative state. You should hear your teammates saying their Power Words throughout the day as well. Hold each other accountable.

TODAY'S ACTION-CHALLENGE

MAGIC JOHNSON

"Manhood is taking care of your family and being able to bless other people. Not yourself— but whether you can bless other people."

"Ask not what your teammates can do for you. Ask what you can do for your teammates."

—Magic Johnson

Day Three

From My Perspective

I was in Los Angeles the day Magic Johnson told the world he was HIV positive. It shocked me and everyone else when they heard the news; back then it was considered a death sentence. He was my favorite NBA player in the eighties, and because I was a point guard, I even put "Magic" on the back of my shirt, as I tried to emulate his game. I admire the way he took responsibility and turned his curse into a blessing. Many would say he has done even more for the world after his Hall of Fame career than he did during it. His story could have gone much differently. What if he had heard that terrible news, given up hope, and simply disappeared and faded away? Many have chosen that path, and nobody would have blamed him—but he's not built that way. He used his ultracompetitive spirit and tackled that challenge the same way he tackled all the others—with pure heart. What is the biggest challenge in your life today? Turn that curse into your blessing; no failure is final, unless you give up.

Fascinating Facts

Magic is a twelve-time NBA All Star, a five-time NBA Champion, and a three-time NBA Most Valuable Player. But what is one of his not-so-well-known accomplishments? He claims to have invented the "high five" while playing at Michigan State University! Magic was known not just for his athletic ability, but also for his magnetic personality and electric leadership style. Can you inspire your teammates today with your energy? Learn the Magic.

Today's Achievements

Today I want you to see how many teammates you can encourage, especially those who rarely receive encouragement. Cheer up one of your players who is down. Pay a little extra attention to a teammate who isn't necessarily a standout player. Use your voice today to inspire your team. Your coaches should notice a difference in you today on the field and in the locker room.

"Leadership is getting players to believe in you. If you tell a teammate you're ready to play as tough as you're able to, you'd better go out there and do it. Players will see right through a phony. And they can tell when you're not giving it all you've got."

"I don't know if I practiced more than anybody, but I sure practiced enough. I still wonder if somebody—somewhere—was practicing more than me."

—Larry Bird

Day Four

From My Perspective

I was a huge Larry Bird fan as well during the eighties. In my opinion, the eighties were the most magical time in the NBA's rich history the classic matchups between the Lakers and the Celtics, or the Celtics and the Pistons and then Michael came on the scene—history. Larry is one of the greatest shooters of all time, but also one of the most intense competitors the game has ever seen. He was known as one of the greatest all-time trash-talkers, but he did it in a way that did not belittle his opponent, or even get the camera's attention. He just got in your head and stole your edge. That takes supreme confidence that only comes from countless hours of practice and repetition. It is said that success is primarily mental, and much less physical than we tend to think it is—especially for the athlete. Would your coaches say that you are mentally tough, or just physically gifted? Show them.

Fascinating Facts

Larry is a twelve-time NBA All Star, a three-time NBA Champion, and a three-time NBA Most Valuable Player. Recruited by Bobby Knight of the legendary Indiana Hoosiers into Indiana University straight from high school, Larry Bird would last only a few weeks before he left—due to not only the strangeness of his new environment, but a severe lack of funds. Larry returned home to French Lick, where he also dropped out of junior college. He took a job with the city as a garbage man out of necessity. In the meantime, he also found himself newly married and with a child. What is the biggest challenge you will face today in order for you to play the game you love? Champions sacrifice and overcome incredible odds.

Today's Achievements

Today I challenge you to share a personal goal with one of your coaches—one of your "stretch" goals. Goals that we keep to ourselves lack power, because we lack accountability. If you really want to grow, then let your team in on what you are trying to accomplish. Let's take it to the next level.

TODAY'S ACTION-CHALLENGE

DAN GABLE

"I never had the fear of getting beat, which is how most people lose . . . they're scared of somebody."

"Once you've wrestled, everything else in life is easy."

—Dan Gable

Day Five

From My Perspective

I never got to watch Dan Gable compete live, but I always knew his name. His reputation was a guy who NEVER lost. Then he went on to take that same "never say die" spirit into coaching. I've always regarded collegiate and Olympic wrestlers as some of the toughest, most determined athletes in sports. The lengths they are willing to go to make weight, overcome injury, endure pain, and outlast their opponent are truly inspiring. The great ones have a never-give-up mindset that often carries on throughout their lives. Toughness isn't a gift, it's an attitude. It is forged by getting knocked down and getting back up so many times it becomes a habit of never quitting, ever. If you can master that habit, then nothing will be able to beat you.

Fascinating Fact

Dan Gable lost only one match in his entire collegiate wrestling career at Iowa State University, his last, and he won an incredible fifteen NCAA Championships as a head coach. His toughness and greatness were forged through adversity. As a little boy, his home life was tough, and he is said to have spent many a night watching out the front window to make sure his family returned home.[3] He channeled that worry into hard work and became one of the greatest wrestlers of all time. Can you channel YOUR adversity into victory?

Today's Achievements

---

[3] Wright Thompson, "The Losses of Dan Gable," *ESPN* The Magazine, August 21, 2013, http://www.espn.com/espn/feature/story/_/page/Dan-Gable/the-losses-dan-gable.

Today I want you to identify one thing that will impede your personal victory or success. It could be a bad habit like procrastination, an unhealthy relationship, your diet or sleeping patterns, or an addiction to social media or video games that is affecting your focus and energy. Be aware of that character flaw and go to work on it. Make one bold move away from that distraction and toward your personal goals.

TODAY'S ACTION-CHALLENGE

"If I'm going to get hit, why let the guy who's going to hit me get the easiest and best shot? I explode into the guy who's trying to tackle me."

"Never die easy. Why run out of bounds and die easy? Make that linebacker pay. It carries into all facets of your life. It's okay to lose, to die, but don't die without trying, without giving it your best."

—Walter Payton

Day Six

From My Perspective

One of my all-time favorite NFL running backs, Walter "Sweetness" Payton, electrified crowds with his balance, strength, and toughness. He rarely tried to avoid defenders, as he would much rather run over you than around you. His signature style showcased legs that never stopped driving and vicious hits relentlessly dealt to linebackers, corners, and safeties. Walter was one of the hardest men to bring down—ever. His off-season training regimen was legendary. He often trained alone because nobody could keep up with him or finish the workouts. He was driven by something deep inside of him that wanted to be the best that's ever been. What drives you? What does it take to bring you down? Life is going to hit you hard. You've got to hit life even harder. That's what Sweetness did, and he did it better than anyone else.

Fascinating Facts

Walter Payton was a nine-time Pro Bowler, a two-time NFL Most Valuable Player, and a Super Bowl Champion. Amazingly, on November 20, 1977, when he broke O. J. Simpson's record for most rushing yards in a single game, Walter was battling the flu. With a fever, and hot and cold flashes throughout the game, Payton ran for an incredible

275 yards.[4] What adversity can you push through today in order to do something you have never done before? Champions overcome—can you?

<u>Today's Achievements</u>

---

[4] Don Pierson, "8. Nov. 20, 1977 Walter Payton, Who Was to Become the National Football League's All-Time Leading Rusher, Runs for a Record 275 Yards against the Minnesota Vikings at the Soldier Field," *Chicago Tribune*, November 1, 1987, published online at http://articles.chicagotribune.com/1987-11-01/sports/8703230678_1_bears-soldier-field-walter-payton.

Today let's work on a powerful technique that all the great ones possess. I want you to practice the art of visualization, and create in your imagination your desired outcome. Example: "I want us to win our region title this season." Now get into a quiet, comfortable setting where you can concentrate without interruption. Turn off your cell phone, music, and media, and close your eyes and clear your mind. I want you to imagine playing at a peak level, and see yourself making big plays. Visualize a winning streak and personal contribution. Feel the emotion you will experience in that moment. Rehearse it in your mind over and over. Imagine the locker room celebration, and now add color and detail. Don't overthink it, just let your mind go in the right direction. Your brain has one limitation: it can't tell the difference between reality and imagination. Use that limitation to your advantage, and just imagine.

TODAY'S ACTION-CHALLENGE

WEEKLY HUDDLE

Week-One Dream Killer:
Promoting a Bullying Spirit

Think of a time when you were bullied. Try to remember exactly how it made you feel. Now think of a time when you witnessed someone else being bullied and wanted to do something about it, but didn't have the courage to take a stand. If you consider it, wouldn't you say the bullying spirit influences many of the things stealing the dreams of the kids at your school? Violence, depression, anxiety, self-harm, drug use, date rape, and even suicide can all be somehow linked to this dangerous game. At the heart of bullying is violence. Violence begins in the mind before it ever plays out physically. You have been chosen to participate in this project and become Ambassadors of Peace at your school. One of the biggest ways you can lead is to help put an end to this cruel and abusive energy in Generation Z school culture.

Discussion Questions

1) Everyone does things for their own reasons. What do you think drives the bully? What are they getting out of it, and why do you think they do it?

2) Why do you think that a large percentage of school bullies happen to be athletes? What would drive the most popular kids in the school to ridicule and dominate the weak?

3) How would you define the word compassion, and why do you think many young people perceive it as a weakness?

4) What are three specific things you could do as leaders at your school to end bullying and shift the school culture toward peace and compassion?

Each week we will collectively grade ourselves as a team on our effort, attitude, and overall intensity this past week. Be honest and hold yourselves to a high standard for excellence. (Your Team Captains will assign the weekly grade.)

Week-One Power Grade: _____

Three Lessons Learned This Week:

O

O

O

WEEK-ONE POPP EXERCISE
Winning team gets "Hope Is the New Dope" gear!

WEEK TWO

*I will not blame anyone for my situation;
I will actively search for solutions.*

Blaming is another weak and pitiful strategy for failure. When we blame others for our current situation, we are saying that YOU, not me, are in control of my fate and destiny. Champions do not blame others for their problems or mistakes; instead, they are quick to take responsibility and control what they CAN control: intensity, attitude, and effort. I can't even imagine any of my sports heroes sitting in front of a microphone at a press conference, after losing a big game, and blaming their linemen. Winners just don't do that—and neither should you.

POPP Power Principle #2
We Find What We Look For.

The brain is the most sophisticated technology on the planet, and there is not a close second. It is the most powerful tool we possess, and it is the original search engine. The brain is a learning machine and a storyteller, and it has been trained through repetition to find that which is most important to us (but not necessarily what is best for us). We have all experienced this phenomenon when we are in the market for a certain type of car. It begins to show up all around us, simply because the brain has quickly learned that it is valuable information for you. It allows new information into the conscious mind, and causes you to NOTICE.

The great ones have trained their brains to actively search for what they desire: victory and success. However, if we constantly focus on what we fear, dread, doubt, or worry about, then we are actively programming our brains to find more of the same. Your supercomputer doesn't judge good or bad, healthy or unhealthy, safe or dangerous. It just pays attention to what you pay attention to, and then creates shortcuts to find it more easily tomorrow. That is why losing is a habit. When we blame others, the brain is paying attention and learning, and it begins to create powerful pathways that allow us to continue to blame in the future as a coping mechanism or a defense strategy. Before long we can be searching for who's to blame, rather than picking up our teammates. The blame game is not a strategy for winning championships, or life for that matter. Take back control today, and look for some new things.

CAUTION FLAG

Pay attention to disrespect in the classroom by your classmates toward your teachers. The first step is awareness. Begin to notice this week.

Watch Week-Two POPP Video

This week we will get into the minds of those who have achieved what few others ever have. This week: **NO BLAMING.** Reclaim your power.

Coaches Corner

Phil Jackson[5]

I so enjoyed watching this man coach the Lakers back in the day. He took a team of superstars and turned them into a cohesive unit that won championships. This was back in the day when trades were rare, and players didn't jump from team to team until they won a ring. The coach had to take the unit he or she had and build a winner. Coach Jackson did that, but he used a unique style and system of techniques. He drew from ancient philosophies to instill in his players a depth of strength and calm that is rare among professional athletes. But when game time came, they were anything but docile—they were pure excitement and energy, but under control. He showed them inspirational movies, had them read significant books, and had deep talks with them, not just about sports, but about life. I want to challenge you this week to look for life lessons in the things your coaches are teaching you. Trust me, you'll remember them some day.

Achievements

Phil Jackson is widely regarded as one of the greatest coaches in the history of the NBA, leading his teams to an

---

[5] Biography.com, s.v. "Phil Jackson," updated February 19, 2016, https://www.biography.com/people/phil-jackson-224897.

incredible eleven league championships—a record that will be very difficult to break. Jackson is known for taking a holistic approach into his coaching, teaching Eastern philosophy and Native American spiritual practices to his players—helping them not just become better players, but better men. In his amazing run with the Chicago Bulls, he led his team to a pair of three-peats winning back-to-back-to-back championships TWICE—an unbelievable feat. Jackson then went on to win five more rings with the Los Angeles Lakers. This Hall of Fame coach was able to lead superstars such as Michael Jordan and Kobe Bryant, and manage a cast of colorful characters around these champions, while bringing out the best in them. He forged unity among his players. Are you helping your coaches build a unified team? Buy in to what they are teaching you—ALL IN.

"As much as we pump iron and we run to build our strength up, we need to build our mental strength up . . . so we can focus . . . so we can be in concert with one another."

"Wisdom is always an overmatch for strength."

"If you meet the Buddha in the lane, feed him the ball."

—Phil Jackson

Week-Two Local Flavor

Coach Matt Dickmann
Harrison Hoyas
Kennesaw, GA

In 2012, while coaching the Seminole Ridge Hawks in Palm Beach County, Florida, Coach Dickmann received five Coach of the Year awards for the area by Nike, the Miami Dolphins, Palm Beach County All-Conference, (*Sun Sentinel),* and (*Palm Beach Post).* In 2016, Coach Dickmann's Harrison Hoyas led the region in most points scored on offense, least points allowed on defense, and broke all eleven team strength records. Dickmann was selected Cobb County Coach of the Year by the *Marietta Daily Journal* and 6A Coach of the Year by the *Atlanta Journal-Constitution*.

Coach's Quote

"Our mission is to stress the importance of education and becoming a better student, to instill the importance of becoming a better person on and off the football field, and to teach the fundamentals of football along with the work ethic needed to succeed. Our football staff believes if our athletes focus on the aspects listed above, our athletes will be successful at Harrison High School and we will be successful as a team."

—Matt Dickmann

"I'm a firm believer in the theory that people only do their best at things they truly enjoy. It is difficult to excel at something you don't enjoy."

"Confidence is the most important single factor in this game, and no matter how great your natural talent, there is only one way to obtain and sustain it: work."

—Jack Nicklaus

Day Seven

From My Perspective

I once met Jack Nicklaus at the wedding of his son Steve. He was a gentleman and carried himself humbly, but with an air of royalty. I will never forget it. He ruled the PGA for decades, and set records that will probably never be broken. He set his sights and goals on winning major championships, and by the time it was over he had won more than anyone. He was the ultimate competitor, and he was driven to beat the best in the world. That's how champions are built—they desire to play the best, and beat the best, for nothing else will do. Do you rise to the level of your competition? Do you compete your best when you face the best? Anyone can beat inferior and weaker opponents, and you should. Champions are forged when tested in the heat of the battle, and they emerge even stronger than before. Rise to the challenge today.

Fascinating Facts

The "Golden Bear" won an unprecedented eighteen major championships, and a total of seventy-three PGA Tour victories. His final major-championship trophy came at the age of forty-six at the 1986 Masters—making Jack the Masters' oldest winner. But here's something you might not know about the PGA's greatest champion: Jack Nicklaus earned a whopping $33.33 for his first tour paycheck in the 1962 Los Angeles Open.[6] Today he is said to be worth an estimated $330 million.[7] Just play the game to the utmost of your ability, and let the prizes and awards worry about themselves.

Today's Achievements

---

[6] John Holmes, "Jack Nicklaus Got His First Pro Check 53 Years Ago Today," PGA.com, January 8, 2015, http://www.pga.com/news/golf-buzz/jack-nicklaus-got-first-pro-check-53-years-ago-today.

[7] "The Good Oil: Pundits Pick Return of Renault Alpine," *New Zealand Herald*, May 19, 2012, http://www.nzherald.co.nz/goodoil/news/article.cfm?c_id=&objectid=10806838.

Today I want you to identify
the weak spot in your game.
What is the most vulnerable area
in your arsenal? Everybody has a
weakness, but many avoid, deny,
or resist that area of their game.
The great ones go to work and
turn that weakness into strength.
Tell a teammate what your
weakness is, and boldly proclaim
that you will overcome it. Call
your shot, and get to work.

WILMA RUDOLPH

"Never underestimate the power of dreams and the influence of the human spirit. We are all the same in this notion: the potential for greatness lives within each of us."

"It doesn't matter what you're trying to accomplish. It's all a matter of discipline. I was determined to discover what life held for me beyond the inner-city streets."

—Wilma Rudolph

Day Eight

From My Perspective

Ever feel like you're too young to make a real difference? Let Wilma Rudolph inspire you. At a time in our nation's history where people of color, and women for that matter, were not respected nor given the equal rights they deserved, Ms. Rudolph used her God-given gifts to inspire not only her classmates, but the whole world. It would have been so easy for her to talk herself out of her greatness: "I'm too young; I'm not the right color; it's not my time yet; I don't have enough help." But she didn't listen to that inner critic. She rose above and found her greatness at a very young age. You can make your mark too, but you need to start NOW.

Fascinating Facts

By the time she was sixteen, Wilma Rudolph had earned a berth on the US Olympic track and field team and came home from the 1956 Melbourne Games to show her high school classmates an Olympic bronze medal. At the 1960 Summer Olympics in Rome, she won three sprint gold medals on a cinder track in the 100m, 200m, and 4 x 100m relay. Not bad for a young athlete who spent her early years in leg braces and wheelchairs, the result of a disability.[8] Because of her attitude, effort, and intensity, Wilma rose above her disability and became an Olympic champion. What obstacles and adversities must you rise above in order to become the athlete you are destined to be? Do not let your challenges define you—rise above.

Today's Achievements

---

[8] "A Life of Foot Deformity Once Faced Swift Wilma," *Tennessean,* September 6, 1960.

Great teams have great relationships. Regardless of color, size, age, or even ability, great teams come together. Today I want you to pick out a player you don't know well or don't get along with. I challenge you to break bread together and get to know each other better. Discover five fascinating facts about each other's life stories. You'll be amazed; we all have a story, and the closer we are as teammates, the stronger we are as a unit—and the farther we'll go together.

TODAY'S ACTION-CHALLENGE

"I've missed more than nine thousand shots in my career. I've lost almost three hundred games. Twenty-six times, I've been trusted to take the game-winning shot and missed. I've failed over and over, and over again in my life. And that is why I succeed."

"Sometimes you need to get hit in the head to realize that you're in a fight."

—Michael Jordan

Day Nine

From My Perspective

I am so grateful that I got to watch Michael Jordan's entire career, from his NCAA championship winning shot to his final NBA game. He broke records, accomplished the nearly impossible "three-peat" (winning back-to-back-to-back NBA championships), retired, made a comeback, and then amazingly won another three-peat (a feat I doubt will ever be accomplished again). But did you know he was cut from the high school basketball team as a sophomore? His coach told him he had the talent, but not the heart. Michael allowed that to motivate him, and then went on to win five NBA Most Valuable Player awards. How do you respond when someone tells you what you cannot do? Does it discourage you, or motivate you? Don't let anyone tell you how great you can or cannot be. Dig deep and find out for yourself.

Fascinating Facts

Michael is a six-time NBA Champion, a five-time NBA Most Valuable Player, and a fourteen-time NBA All Star. Many recognize Jordon for his signature habit on the court: sticking his tongue out while dazzling opponents with out-of-this-world moves. Legend has it that he picked up the habit while watching his father working and fixing things around the house. His father claimed that it went back even farther, as he had watched his grandfather stick his tongue out while concentrating on his chores![9] Pay attention to your role models today, because you are picking up their habits too—the good ones AND the bad ones.

Today's Achievements

[9] Lazenby, Ronald. *Michael Jordan: The Life*. New York: Little, Brown and Company, 2014.

Today I want you to do something special for a parent or guardian. It can be a card, a text, a voicemail, or preferably a hug. Let them know how grateful you are for their love and support that has allowed you to grow to the point where you are a competitor and an athlete. Regardless of the current state of your relationship, make a decision to show them love today. You wouldn't be here if it weren't for them bringing you into this world. Show them you appreciate their role, big or small, in providing you with what you have and who you are. If it is not possible to do this with family, then share it with a coach or teacher who has played a big role in your life. Gratitude is a powerful, winning energy.

TODAY'S ACTION-CHALLENGE

"The idea is not to block every shot. The idea is to make your opponent believe that you might block every shot."

"Concentration and mental toughness are the margins of victory."

—Bill Russell

Day Ten

From My Perspective

I met Bill Russell when I was a kid, but never got to watch him play, as he was before my time. But I can tell you this: there has never been, in my opinion, a greater winner in the history of the game. All he did was win championships—eight in a row! Can you imagine the pressure of being and staying on top for that long? He was a true leader, made all his teammates better, and led by example on the court. His team reflected his heart. Winning is a habit, something you come to expect. However, so is losing. Winning is contagious, but it takes a spark. Be that spark today for your team—who knows how bright it will burn.

Fascinating Facts

Russell is a twelve-time NBA All Star, a five-time NBA Most Valuable Player, and incredibly, an eleven-time NBA Champion. Recognized as one of the greatest winners of all time, Bill could have easily settled for less. As a boy, Russell battled several different illnesses that made him what many would consider a "sickly child." He also faced his share of racism and segregation growing up in the South, before his father relocated them to Oakland,

California, where he found work at a shipyard.[10] Do you have someone in your life who has sacrificed in order for you to have the opportunities you have today? Work like you appreciate them.

Today's Achievements

[10] Biography.com, s.v. "Bill Russell," updated February 4, 2016, https://www.biography.com/people/bill-russell-9467384.

Today you will speak somewhere in the neighborhood of ten thousand to fifteen thousand words. Words are powerful and creative, whether they are positive or negative. I want you to be aware of every word that comes out of your mouth today. Just witness and observe without judgment. Try to determine if those words are making you more powerful, or if they are stealing your power. Also pay attention to the words of your teammates and friends. You'll be amazed at the percentage of wasted words and careless speech. Be deliberate and create victory through your language.

"*You can't just beat a team, you have to leave a lasting impression in their minds so they never want to see you again.*"

"*The vision of a champion is bent over, drenched in sweat, at the point of exhaustion, when nobody else is looking.*"

—Mia Hamm

Day Eleven

From My Perspective

I began playing soccer when I was six and gave it up when I was twenty. I loved it. However, growing up, it was popular with boys, but the best female athletes played basketball, volleyball, softball, and tennis. Mia Hamm changed all that. Little girls had a role model and something to shoot for. What if she hadn't done the most with her gift? I imagine somebody else would have done it, but they didn't and she did. Why not do something that's never been done before? Everything is impossible until someone does it. Take another look at the goals you set at the beginning of this project. Stretch yourself, and strive for even more.

Fascinating Facts

Mia Hamm is listed as one of the 125 best living soccer players. She held the record for most international goals until 2013, and she still holds the national team record for most assists. She is also in the National Soccer Hall of Fame. Gifted and athletic from an early age, Mia often competed with the boys, and often beat them. However, it didn't come easy for her. She was born with a club foot, and she had to wear a cast and then corrective footwear in order to correct the defect.[11] Ironically, her feet would get her all the way to the Hall of Fame. What is your best excuse?

Today's Achievements

---

[11] CNN Programs: People in the News, hosted by Paula Zahn, "Soccer Star Raising Goals in Women's Sports," Mia Hamm Profile, CNN.com, accessed August 22, 2017, http://www.cnn.com/CNN/Programs/people/shows/hamm/profile.html.

Today I want you to imagine there's a secret camera following you around 24/7, recording every move (kind of like they do during your games on Friday nights). Become aware of your daily actions: how you walk, how you talk, who you hang out with, what gets your valuable attention, how you invest your precious time. It's time to start thinking like a role model— because people ARE watching.

"I let my feet spend as little time on the ground as possible. From the air, fast down, and from the ground, fast up."

"We all have dreams. But in order to make dreams come into reality, it takes an awful lot of determination, dedication, self-discipline, and effort."

—Jesse Owens

Day Twelve

From My Perspective

Great athletes keep their head under extreme pressure. Can you imagine having the eyes of the whole world upon you with a world war brewing, as a black man, in front of one of the most evil men who ever lived as he tries to humiliate you on a global scale? Jesse Owens not only finished, but he dominated. He thrived when the weight of the world was on his shoulders. I admire a man like that. You can learn to handle whatever pressure life throws at you, but it will take maximum effort and tremendous heart. Is it in you? I believe it is.

Fascinating Facts

Jesse Owens has often been called the greatest athlete in track-and-field history. He once broke three world records, and tied another, in less than an hour (1935 Big Ten Track Meet, Ann Arbor, Michigan). However, it was his four gold medals at the 1936 Olympic Games in Berlin that would launch him into legendary status. At the peak of the Third Reich's myth of Aryan supremacy, and with Adolf Hitler in attendance, Owens won the 100m, 200m, long jump, and 4x100m relay. [12] How do you handle pressure?

Today's Achievements

[12] International Olympic Committee. 2017. "Jesse Owens." Olympic Games. Accessed September 18, 2017. https://www.olympic.org/jesse-owens.

Today I want you to think of something you really want. Choose something you want to build, achieve, obtain, create, discover, develop, or experience. Don't worry about how, who, or even when. Just focus on what and WHY. Now, share it with a friend or a coach, and make a move in that direction—take action, even if it's just a small step, in the direction of your dream.

WEEKLY HUDDLE

Week-Two Dream Killer: Irresponsible Social Media

Social media has forever changed our world. However, as with every technological advancement, it can be used for good and noble purposes, or to harm people. Companies, colleges, and professional teams now have divisions and full-time positions created to research your social media before recruiting or hiring you. The reason? It shows them your character, your judgment, and your maturity level. However, there are even more important reasons for you to pay careful attention to the things you share and post. Many people watch what you do and what you deem important. Whether you like it or not, you are a role model, and you have more influence at your school than most. One careless post or joke about a classmate can have significant consequences. You never know what that person is going through on a personal level, and what might push them over the edge. Use your influence intentionally and deliberately.

Discussion Questions

1) How would you define social-media addiction? By that definition, would you say you are possibly addicted?

2) Share a real-life example of someone who was harmed at your school by reckless social-media usage (no names, please).

3) Discuss how irresponsible social-media use could negatively affect your future. Give specific examples of how someone

could ruin future opportunities by being careless in this area.

4) Collectively, you probably have more followers than any other students at your school. What are three things you could do as a team that would create a whole new positive energy around social-media norms?

Week-Two Power Grade: _____

Three Lessons Learned This Week:

○

○

○

WEEK-TWO POPP EXERCISE
Winning team gets "Hope Is the New Dope" gear!

WEEK THREE

*I will not make excuses for my problems
or mistakes; I will take action.*

Making excuses is yet another game plan for defeat. What is your most sophisticated excuse? You know, the one you pull out when you lose battles that you really should have won. Typically, it's a sad story of something done to you or taken from you. For many, making excuses has become an unconscious strategy along the way for dealing with painful losses. However, if you want to go on a winning streak and sustain it, then you must break this destructive and powerless habit. Own the loss, accept the lessons, and learn from it with even greater resolve. Dropping excuses is liberating, because you are taking back your personal power and controlling the things you can control.

POPP Power Principle #3
We Find That Which Is Like Ourselves.

We've all heard the saying "Birds of a feather flock together." This is very true. Actually, it's an energy thing. At our most fundamental level, we are made of pure energy. We tend to be drawn to people who have similar energy patterns and vibrations. We see this in friendships, clubs, cliques, gangs, and even romance—powerful attractions.

This is a powerful dynamic with team sports. Dominant energy frequencies affect the chemistry and momentum of the whole team. Making excuses becomes a habit and steals the power from your team. Great teams don't make excuses, but rather make adjustments and take action. Once again, making excuses is nothing more than building your case for failure before you even get there—it is quite literally a strategy for defeat. Be careful who gets your time, energy, and focus. Winners hang with winners, or have the extraordinary energy to turn losers into champions.

CAUTION FLAG

Pay attention to the leaders on your team this week. Watch how your teammates are following their lead. The first step is awareness—simply notice this week.

Watch Week-Three POPP Video

This week we will get into the minds of those who have achieved what few others ever have. This week: **NO EXCUSES**. Reclaim your power.

Coaches Corner

Tony Dungy

Tony Dungy was not just a coach; he was a spiritual leader for his players. I would go so far as to say he taught them as much about how to be good men as how to play football. That's the kind of coach I want—one who cares just as much about me as a person as they do a player. And his players rose to the challenge. He took teams who were mediocre at best and turned them into champions. I want you to notice and appreciate this week how much your coaches sacrifice for you: they choose to give up time with their families; they show up early and stay late; they often must miss dinnertime, and sometimes even vacations . . . They care about you and show it every day, so please act accordingly.

Achievements

Tony Dungy, along with his superstar quarterback Peyton Manning, turned the Indianapolis Colts into a perennial championship contender. Dungy became the first African American coach to win a Super Bowl, winning the Lombardy Trophy on February 4, 2007. He also became just the third person in the history of the NFL to win the title as a player and a head coach. Tony is more than a player and a coach; he is a father, a husband, a brother, a friend, a son, and a role model to many. Are you a positive or a negative role model to those watching you?

"When you're in a situation, you can complain about it, you can feel sorry for yourself, you can do a lot of things. But how are you gonna make the situation better?"

"You should never be defined by what you do, by the things you have; you've got to define yourself by who you are and who you impact, and how you impact people. And that's the thing I try to get across to my players."

—Tony Dungy

Week-Three Local Flavor

Coach Matthew Combs
Alexander Cougars
Douglasville, GA

Coach Combs is now in his nineteenth year of coaching, and has spent the last eight years as the head coach at Alexander High School. During that stretch, Combs has taken his teams to the state playoffs four years in a row (first time in school history); he was named Douglas County Coach of the Year in 2013 and 2014; and Coach Combs was elected Positive Athlete Coach of the

Year for the state of Georgia in 2014. Combs has coached thirteen All-State player selections, nine of those 1st Team All-State.

Coach's Quote

"The reason most people fail, instead of succeed, is that they trade what they want the most for what they want in the moment."

—Matthew Combs

PELÉ

"Success is no accident. It is hard work, perseverance, learning, studying, sacrifice, and most of all, love of what you are doing or learning to do."

"Enthusiasm is everything. It must be taut and vibrating like a guitar string."

—Pelé

Day Thirteen

From My Perspective

One of the high points of my young soccer career was getting my idol Pelé's autograph. I treasured it. I wanted to play like him. I watched him play in the latter part of his career, learned how to do a bicycle kick because of him, and even took his number ten as my own and wore it all the way into college. I imitated his game and practiced his moves. He created a special style, which was at first rejected, and then embraced—and it changed the game worldwide. Someone once said imitation is the sincerest form of flattery. Who are you following today? Which athletes are you studying and imitating? You become like those you spend the most time with, so choose wisely.

Fascinating Facts

Widely regarded as one of the greatest soccer players of all time, Pelé has also been said to have been the first one who used the phrase "The Beautiful Game" for soccer. In 1999 Pelé was elected "Athlete of the Century" by the IOC, and was named to the list of "100 Most Influential People" by *Time* magazine. [13] Pelé scored an astounding 129 "hat tricks" in his brilliant career. It is quite an accomplishment

---

[13] "Pele: One of the Greatest Footballers of All Time," All American Entertainment, accessed August 22, 2017, http://allamericanentertainment.com/speakers/pele.

for a player to score three goals in a game at least once in their career. Pelé did it not once, but 129 times! Here's a question for you: If you gave it 100 percent on the court, on the field, and in the training room, how far could you go? You'll never find out until you give it your all.

Today's Achievements

I want you to think of your most sophisticated excuse. You know, the one you pull out when things don't go your way, or when you fail. "I'm too young; I'm too small; I'm not as strong as he is; I'm not fast enough; Coach doesn't like me; things aren't good at home . . ." What's your BEST excuse? Make a decision today that you are going to drop that weight from around your neck. Let it go. If you really want to take it to the next level, then share it with your coach or training partner.

"I hated every minute of training, but I said, 'Don't quit. Suffer now and live the rest of your life as a champion.'"

"He who is not courageous enough to take risks will accomplish nothing in life."

—Muhammad Ali

Day Fourteen

From My Perspective

Muhammad Ali made me into a boxing fan. I can remember staying up late and watching his fights as a kid. His brilliance, humor, physical talent, and skill were mesmerizing. But it was his courage that moved me. He stood up for what he believed in, even though it cost him dearly. His crowning moment happened in my hometown of Atlanta as he lit the Olympic flame at the opening of the 1996 Games. Tears filled my eyes as he stood there proudly in front of the whole world, trembling, as the signs of his Parkinson's disease had become quite evident. One day you will look back on your life and see all that you stood for. The choices you make on this day, you will most definitely care about someday in the future when you become a husband, a father, a wife, or a mother. Make wise choices—they really do matter, and you really will care.

Fascinating Facts

Born and raised in Louisville, Kentucky, Cassius Clay won a gold medal in the light heavyweight division at the 1960 Summer Olympics in Rome. He turned professional the same year. After converting to Islam and changing his name to Muhammad Ali, he refused to be drafted into the military because of his religious beliefs and because he opposed the war in Vietnam. He was arrested, found guilty of draft evasion, and stripped of his boxing titles (he successfully appealed the decision and his conviction was overturned four years later). As a conscientious objector, Ali became a counterculture icon and a voice for change in America. Ali was named among the "Greatest Athletes of the Twentieth Century" by ESPN.[14]

Today's Achievements

---

[14] ESPN. "Top N. American athletes of the century." ESPN.com. Accessed September 18, 2017. http://www.espn.com/sportscentury/athletes.html.

Okay, it's time to become even more aware of the information you are downloading into your headspace. Today I want you to pay attention to the information you're taking in: your music, your video games, your social media, your television, your magazines. No judgment, just observation. Your brain is always paying attention to what you're paying attention to. Now answer this question honestly: is this information making you stronger, or taking away your power? Guard your mind and regain your personal power. Delete the negative information and unhealthy influences in your life.

"You just can't beat the person who never gives up."

"Never let the fear of striking out get in your way."

"Every strike brings me closer to the next home run."

—Babe Ruth

Day Fifteen

From My Perspective

You might wonder why I put Babe Ruth in this book. You've probably heard all the things that made him the wrong kind of role model (one way or another, we are all role models). Babe Ruth did not have a happy childhood. He and his sister were the only children out of eight siblings who survived infancy. He was sent to an orphanage by his father at age seven. For twelve years, he rarely saw his family, not on holidays nor the Sunday per month designated for visitors. He became an unruly student. He eventually started to turn his life around when he found a father figure in Brother Matthias at the St. Mary's School. He became an inspiration to Babe in baseball, as well as life in general.[15] So, what is your best excuse? Do you have it tough? Give it up, and focus on what you CAN control. Drop your excuses, and BECOME.

Fascinating Facts

As the all-time home-run leader, Babe Ruth held the most coveted record in baseball for over fifty-two years. Ruth was the American League ERA leader (pitching) in 1916, AL MVP in 1923, AL Batting Champion in 1924,

---

[15] Babe Ruth Central, "Ruth's Childhood," BR3 Enterprises, accessed August 22, 2017, http://www.baberuthcentral.com/babe-ruth-biography/ruths-childhood/.

and a seven-time World Series Champion. However, Babe didn't start life as a winner. Drinking and chewing tobacco by the age of eight, Babe was sent to a Catholic reform school, and had the reputation of a wild and unruly child.[16] Sports helped him find the focus and drive to turn his life around, though he "lived large" throughout his colorful career. Who knows where the New York Yankees would be as a franchise today if they hadn't gotten "The Babe" from their rival Red Sox Maybe your life could be a comeback story too.

Today's Achievements

---

[16] Ibid.

Today let's demonstrate the power of mantras and affirmations. Choose a power statement that you will carry with you and repeat throughout the day. It doesn't have to be drawn out or complicated; in fact, simple is better. Examples: "I am happy, healthy, joyous, and free," or "In everything and every way, I'm getting stronger every day," or "I'm a champion, and I ALWAYS finish strong." Say it with passion, and say it again and again until you believe it. Pay attention—you'll be amazed what happens to your energy.

TODAY'S ACTION-CHALLENGE

"I loved the game. We played because we loved it."

"Success is not only for the elite. Success is there for those who want it, plan for it, and take action to achieve it."

—Jim Brown

Day Sixteen

From My Perspective

Jim Brown was one of the most dominant athletes in any sport, of any era. He broke and set all the NFL individual rushing records at the time while only playing nine seasons, and in an era when there were only twelve regular-season games. With no more records to break, he walked away on his own terms—healthy, secure, and eventually a Hall of Famer. If he had continued playing, he most likely would have set records that would've never been broken. Obviously, he played for the love of the game, and not for individual accolades. Are you willing to put the good of the team ahead of yourself? That's what true leaders do. Discover your true gift, and play your specific role to the best of your ability. Give it your all, and let the stats take care of themselves.

Fascinating Facts

Jim Brown is a nine-time Pro Bowler, three-time NFL Most Valuable Player, and 1964 NFL Champion. After his retirement from the NFL, Brown went on to have a long and distinguished acting career, appearing in over forty films. In 1988, Brown founded the Amer-I-Can Program. Operating in inner cities and prisons, he currently works with juveniles who have gotten involved in the gang life in

Los Angeles and Cleveland.[17] Believe in your teammates, no matter where they happen to be along their journey. Everybody needs a second chance.

<u>Today's Achievements</u>

---

[17] Thomson Gale, s.v. "Jim Brown," *Contemporary Black Biography* (Detroit, MI: Gale Research, 2005).

One of your teammates is struggling today. Somebody is having a tough time. Regardless of the reason, they didn't come to play. Figure out who it is, and cheer them up. We all need a lift every now and then, but first you must NOTICE. Your team is only as strong as its weakest link. Locate that link and strengthen it today. That's what leaders do.

WAYNE GRETZKY

"Procrastination is one of the most common and deadliest of diseases, and its toll on success and happiness is heavy."

"The highest compliment that you can pay me is to say that I work hard every day, that I never dog it."

—Wayne Gretzky

Day Seventeen

From My Perspective

Being from the South, I did not grow up a hockey fan. But I was a Wayne Gretzky fan, because he was absolutely the greatest hockey player who ever lived—and most would say there isn't a close second. By all accounts, he wasn't naturally gifted in terms of size or speed, but he made up for it in his work ethic. We all have God-given gifts and talents, but only the great ones maximize those talents. It would have been a shame if Wayne had not pushed himself to his limit. The world would have missed out on watching "The Great One," as he was known. What will you do with your talent? It would be a such a waste of your gifts if you didn't maximize your potential. Get after it today—it's all we ever have.

Fascinating Facts

Nicknamed the "Great One," Wayne Gretzky is widely regarded as the best hockey player of all time. At the time of his retirement in 1999, he held an astounding sixty-one NHL records. One of his many records includes having the most NHL career points—2,857. However, check this: Even if he had never scored a single one of his amazing 894 goals, he would still be the league's all-time leading scorer. How? All those assists—1,963 of them. That's right, the Great One wasn't just great individually. He was an incredible offensive player who helped his entire team achieve success.

Today's Achievements

Today I want you to be a peacemaker. Keep an eye out for someone who is in a vulnerable position or a bad situation. Get involved, when appropriate, and try to bring peace and reconciliation. Be a role model for peace today in your community. Somebody needs help, and you might be the only person who sees it.

"I didn't say I was that smart, I said I went to class and I enjoyed what I was doing."

"Maybe I was born to play ball. Maybe I truly was."

—Willie Mays

Day Eighteen

From My Perspective

Willie Mays did it all: he was an All Star for his defense, his hitting, his base stealing, his arm . . . he excelled in every aspect of the game. I love watching clips of him in the outfield; there was almost no ball hit that he couldn't get to. And he would sacrifice his body to make unbelievable, circus-like catches in center field. He played ALL OUT (today we would say he had a great "motor"). How much of your heart have you given to your game? Is there still gas left in the tank? You will be amazed to learn how much more your body can do when it is pushed by a strong mind and a big heart. We live once—give it everything you've got.

Fascinating Facts

Willie Mays was a twenty-four-time All Star, two-time National League MVP, National League batting champion, and 1954 World Series Champion. Willie's parents were both outstanding athletes, and were only sixteen years old when he was born. Willie's dad was a semi-pro baseball player, and his mother was a high school track star. As a matter of fact, even his grandfather pitched in the Negro leagues.[18] Mays was blessed with extraordinary genes! What can you accomplish with gifts that have been passed down to you?

<u>Today's Achievements</u>

---

[18] Linge, Mary Kay. *Willie Mays: A Biography.* Westport, CT: Greenwood Press, 2005.

Today I want to challenge you to use your social media to inspire your followers. Post or share something uplifting, inspirational, and motivational. Watch and see how your community responds. Pay attention to what your teammates post as well, and hold one another accountable. Use your influence for peace—your people are most certainly watching.

TODAY'S ACTION-CHALLENGE

WEEKLY HUDDLE

Week-Three Dream Killer: Objectifying Classmates

Our Creator made us all beautiful and unique: different colors, shapes, sizes, gifts, and talents. We are to honor everything He has made and treat people how we wish to be treated. Imagine how it feels to seem "different" from other kids at this challenging age in your development. All of us go through times when we feel awkward or that we just don't fit in. However, most of you have been gifted with special talents and abilities that set you apart and afford you certain privileges, ones I'm sure you enjoy. Unfortunately, many gifted athletes end up using their God-given talents to satisfy their own desires, rather than to help others. I'm sure you will agree it is never right to use your influence to treat other students as objects rather than fellow human beings. When we treat others as objects, typically we use people in three ways: vehicles, obstacles, or irrelevant. This is very prevalent with teenagers.

Vehicles: People are a means to get what you want or take you where you want to go.

Obstacles: People are getting in the way of what you want or where you want to go.

Irrelevant: People are of no use to you, because they cannot get you what you want, or take you where you want to go.

The obvious and most dangerous form of objectification is using another student to satisfy your sexual desires. Date rape is becoming an epidemic, and sadly, many times it is perpetrated by athletes. You are better than that, I know you are. Let us put an end to it at your school.

Discussion Questions

1) What does it mean to objectify another person? What do you think I mean by treating people as vehicles, obstacles, or irrelevant?

2) It is believed that as many as one in five females will experience unwanted sexual contact by the time they get out of college. Why do you think that percentage is on the rise, and why do you think so many athletes are being charged?

3) Discuss the current "viral video" culture among your generation. What drives it, and why do you think kids today are more concerned with likes and shares than helping those in need?

4) What are three things you could do as a team to protect your weak and vulnerable classmates?

Week-Three Power Grade: _____

Three Lessons Learned This Week:

O

O

O

WEEK-THREE POPP EXERCISE
Winning team gets "Hope Is the New Dope" gear!

WEEK FOUR

*I will not be a victim; I will take
100 percent responsibility for my
life, no matter who is at fault.*

Our country is filled with more and more people who have adopted a "victim mentality." We live in a day and age where fewer and fewer people take responsibility for their lives, and more people than ever feel entitled to success without the necessary work and sacrifice. This book is filled with examples of men and women who refused to complain, blame, or make excuses, and instead took their talents and made the most of them. Why give others the power to control your outcomes? You, and you alone, are solely responsible for your effort and attitude. Don't give that away.

POPP Power Principle #4
What We Focus on Expands, and What We Resist Persists.

We all have unlimited energy that we expend on whatever gets our valuable time and focus. Think of personal energy as your fuel tank, which you are always either filling or draining. We must choose carefully what enters and remains in our headspace if we want to achieve extraordinary success. The brain is always paying attention to what you are paying attention to with no judgment, just observation. It is designed to compound whatever gets most of your attention. This is why a bad day seems to get worse, and it also explains losing streaks and why they are sometimes so hard to break (perhaps it's because we are still focusing on the mistakes and bad breaks that brought about that first loss). If we focus on what we dislike and on things outside our control, then we exaggerate the mistakes and missteps, strengthen our opponents, and enlarge our obstacles. Instead, focus on proper techniques, game plans, and positive visualization. Do not waste energy resisting things outside your control. You cannot control the officials, the crowd, bad breaks, weather, or the other team, for that matter. Control what you CAN control: attitude and effort.

CAUTION FLAG

Pay attention to the way your friends talk about the opposite sex this week. Don't judge or preach, simply notice. The first step is awareness, so pay attention.

Watch Week-Four POPP Video

This week we will get into the minds of those who have achieved what few others ever have. This week: **NO VICTIMS**. Reclaim your power.

Coaches Corner

Pat Summitt[19]

Pat Summitt struck fear into the hearts of opposing teams (whether they admitted it or not). NOBODY wanted to play Tennessee when she was in her prime—which was a long stretch. Her players were intensely loyal to her, and they completely bought into her system. She convinced them that if they bought into her philosophy as a team, they would win championships. And they did. Do you trust your coaches? Or do you think you know better? This week I want you to put aside all preconceived notions and prejudices, and TOTALLY buy in to what your coaches are teaching, not just about your technique, but about their overall philosophy. You want to win? Trust your coaches.

Achievements

Pam Summitt was raised on a dairy farm and first played basketball in a hayloft. Perhaps that is where her toughness, grit, and determination spring from. Summitt was well known for her tough practices, high standards for excellence, and her legendary "look" that kept her players in check. Coach Summitt went on to lead her Tennessee Lady Volunteers to eight NCAA Women's Basketball titles, and became the first NCAA basketball coach in history with one thousand career wins. In 1998, she led Tennessee to an unprecedented third straight NCAA Championship, and a perfect 39-0 record. Coach Summitt

---

[19] The Pat Summitt Foundation. "Her Story." The Pat Summitt Foundation. Accessed September 18, 2017.
http://www.patsummitt.org/our_role/pats_story/her_story.aspx.

only did things one way: Total Commitment. Do you demand excellence from yourself and your teammates?

"Winning is fun . . . Sure. But winning is not the point. Wanting to win is the point. Not giving up is the point. Never letting up is the point. Never being satisfied with what you've done is the point."

"We keep score in life because it matters. It counts. It matters. Too many people opt out and never discover their own abilities because they fear failure. They don't understand commitment."

—Pat Summitt

Week-Four Local Flavor

Coach Gary Varner
Allatoona Buccaneers
Acworth, GA

Coach Varner's coaching highlights include serving as the offensive coordinator at Roswell High School for three seasons where the Hornets went 32-7-1, including a 7-2-1 playoff record, and a State Championship in 2006. Coach Varner is now leading Allatoona into their tenth season, where he has compiled a record of 72-21 and has led his Bucs to the state playoffs for the last six years, including two trips to the quarter finals, a trip to the state semifinals, and a State Championship in 2015.

Fascinating Fact

Coach Varner served five years in the US Navy on board the USS *Truxton* as a nuclear-reactor operator.

Coach's Quote

"The key to success is committing to the process. You never arrive at anything quickly in life you have to be willing to embrace the step-by-step journey toward the finish line."

—Gary Varner

"Once that bell rings you're on your own. It's just you and the other guy."

"You need a lot of different types of people to make the world better."

—Joe Louis

Day Nineteen

From My Perspective

It's hard to become a champion, but even harder to stay there. Once you become number one, you have a big target on your back: Everybody wants a shot at the title, and everyone wants your crown. Joe Louis kept the most coveted belt in the world for an astounding twelve years, during a time in our nation's history when it was difficult to succeed as a person of color. Winning streaks are a magical thing in sports, and momentum is a powerful force. It takes incredible work ethic, a little bit of luck, and sheer determination. You got some of that? Start your personal winning streak today.

Fascinating Facts

Joe Louis, nicknamed the "Brown Bomber," reigned as heavyweight champion from 1937 all the way to 1949, an incredible accomplishment. His is widely considered one of the greatest boxers in the history of the sport, and *Ring* magazine listed him as one of the "100 greatest punchers of all time." Louis successfully defended his title twenty-five times—second all time. Joe Louis broke the color barrier and began a wave that would eventually open all of big-league sports to black athletes. Eventually Joe would become a celebrity, black hero, and sports icon. When he died, millions mourned his passing. It's been said that Muhammad Ali stated, "Everybody cried."[20]

Today's Achievements

---

[20] Dana R. Barnes, s.v. Joe Louis, *Notable Sports Figures* (Farmington Hills, MI: Gale Group, 2004).

Today I want you to show up early to practice and stay late. Work on a weakness and set an example of your dedication to your team's success. Your coaches and peers will notice your commitment and follow suit. If you are already doing that, which I hope you are, then come a little earlier, and stay even later. Time to push your greatness to a new limit. We make time for the things most important us.

JACKIE JOYNER-KERSEE

"It's better to look ahead and prepare, than to look back and regret."

"I have this burning desire to get out there and do my best. It's as if I'm keeping it all in a little bottle, and it's all going to come out when I do the best I'm capable of doing."

—Jackie Joyner-Kersee

Day Twenty

From My Perspective

I've been a fan of the Olympic Games for as long as I can remember. I love seeing athletes who have prepared for years, on the world's biggest stage and competing against the very best with only a few minutes to perform. Their entire career will be judged by how they handle those few, precious moments. Talk about pressure. Now imagine having to be the best in a half-dozen different events! Can you imagine all the countless hours of blood, sweat, and tears that go into that kind of training? No wonder many called Jackie Joyner-Kersee the greatest female athlete of all time. To be great, you have to be stellar in every aspect of your game. When you compete against the best, weak spots in your game will be exposed and tested. Make a decision today that you will master the areas of your craft that are your current weaknesses. This is work behind the scenes that no one will ever see—but it will be revealed under the spotlight.

Fascinating Facts

Jackie excelled in the long jump and the heptathlon. She medaled in those two events at four different Olympic Games. *Sports Illustrated for Women* magazine voted Joyner-Kersee the Greatest Female Athlete of All Time. However, it was pain and struggle that formed a champion.

Born to teenage parents, Jackie's family struggled to get by. *Sports Illustrated* wrote, "Their house was little more than wallpaper and sticks, with four tiny bedrooms. During the winters, when the hot-water pipes would freeze, they had to heat water for baths in kettles on the kitchen stove. Their great-grandmother lived with them until she died on the plastic-covered sofa in the living room while Jackie was at the store buying milk." Joyner-Kersee also has battled and overcome asthma throughout her life, and is an inspiration to many.[21]

Today's Achievements

---

[21] Thomson Gale, s.v. "Jackie Joyner-Kersee," *Contemporary Black Biography*.

Today I want you to pick your favorite quote from this project so far and commit it to memory. Now I want you to share it with as many teammates and coaches as you can in one day. Let's see which player can inspire the most people. You are creating a new story that you are going to tell the world. Put it on BLAST.

YOUR HEART IS THE STRONGEST MUSCLE IN YOUR BODY.

Participate in our life-changing 40 Days of Power program and get to work changing some lives of your own.

PowerOfPeaceProject.com

Halftime Locker Room Talk

During every halftime, the coach gets his or her team together in the locker room to make adjustments. What are we doing well, and what do we need to do better? What is the opposition doing well or poorly? Who needs to keep it up, and who needs to step it up? Now it is time for us to evaluate how we did in the first half. Be honest and grade yourself on attitude, effort, and intensity in the first half of this campaign. Now, let's make some adjustments.

Winners maintain keen and clear focus when others are losing their heads. You want to be a game changer? Learn to focus like the most amazing warriors on the planet.

GAMS is a simple acronym I created after researching Navy SEAL training techniques, and especially the process that was developed to help more SEAL candidates survive "Hell Week." The goal is to finish the drill, never give up, and never, EVER ring the bell (the means by which you "give up and go home" in front of all your SEAL candidates). These principles and this process are an effective way of maintaining a high level of intensity during training, and also to maximize your skills, talent, and performance when you are under extreme pressure. All great athletes practice these in one form or another, even if they are unaware of the terms or process itself.

Hell Week is one of the most grueling tests of physical endurance ever created. It is designed to take an individual to the edge of insanity, exhaustion, and even death to see if you will quit—the stakes are too high to have quitters on this team. Those who make it through this phase are truly the elite, the best of the best.

GAMS Training
Goal Setting

Because too many of the candidates were dropping out during Hell Week (a grueling test of human endurance), this system was implemented in order to increase its success rate. First, we must set goals. However, most times the goals were too vague and general (e.g., "Don't give up, don't quit"). Instead, candidates are taught to set short, attainable goals that can carry them through the day (e.g., "Make it through 10:00 a.m. without quitting"). Instructors found that the brain could handle suffering more effectively if the goals were made more "bite sized." And sure enough, more candidates began finishing the drill without ringing the bell.

What are your goals in your specific training routine? Is it your time in the forty-yard dash? Is it your bench press or squat max? Is it your fastball mph? Or maybe your vertical leap or time in the mile? However your sport measures excellence, break it down to attainable measures and then go after it with all your heart while tracking your progress, celebrating victories, and learning from failures. Then when the heat is up on Friday night, you won't ring the bell.

Arousal Control

What is said to be the most intense part of Hell Week is the underwater training. The brain naturally freaks out when it feels like it is drowning. Candidates are weighted and told to go to the bottom of the pool, sit with their breathing apparatus intact, and wait for further instructions. Then the trainer dives to the bottom and rips off the oxygen mask, tangles up the hose, and throws it to the bottom. The candidate, who is blindfolded, must calmly search for the mask and hose, untangle it, and put it back on correctly. Once the oxygen is flowing again, they must wait patiently, only to have it ripped off and tangled up again. This continues as long as the trainer wishes, and if the candidate comes up before the drill is finished, then he must ring the bell and go home.

It was during this drill when many of the candidates were dropping out. The problem is that when an individual is under extreme pressure or anxiety, the body produces stress hormones and adrenaline, which affects blood pressure, temperature, breathing, and mental clarity. In order to perform under pressure, we must be able to control the arousal response. So the candidates are trained to measure and control their breathing, which helps them stay relaxed and in control so they can complete the task without panicking and swimming to the surface for air. This same principle applies when a player must slow everything down in the heat of a strenuous battle, and calmly make two pressure-packed free throws when the game is on the line and the crowd is going wild. It's all about arousal control.

Mental Rehearsal

Science is proving that visualization and imagination are as important, or even more so, than the physical practice itself. Obviously, repetition of the right techniques over time creates muscle memory and leads to subconscious pathways that lead to peak physical performance. As has been said, "Perfect practice makes perfect." However, when the game is on the line, you need mental toughness and quiet, calm focus. That doesn't happen through physical training alone. When an athlete visualizes shooting a free throw, or running a particular play, the exact muscle groups fire, in the same sequence, that would fire if he or she was physically running the play.

Activating your powerful imagination allows the body and mind to connect and align, and the athlete can actually practice and train without moving a muscle or even being on the court or field. In the heat of battle, the body instinctively knows what to do because it believes it has "been there before." A basketball player exhibits just as much improvement by mentally shooting perfect free throws than when the same athlete spends hours actually shooting at the basket. Go there in your mind first, and your body will follow. This alone helped more SEAL candidates survive this grueling ordeal.

Self-Talk

The importance of healthy and powerful self-talk cannot be overstated. What if a place kicker has a "mind virus" that tells him, "Whatever you do, don't hook it left. That is what you did last time." All the brain hears is "Hook it left" and typically that is what happens—a dreaded case of the "yips" can result. Negative self-talk was costing many promising SEAL candidates a shot at their dreams because they had not learned to manage their internal voice. "I can't do this. This is too hard. Nobody would blame me if I quit; lots of guys have quit. The pain is too much. If it gets any harder, I'm done." Sound familiar? The chances of you succeeding with that head trash is slim to none. What if instead this is the internal dialogue for someone going through the exact same test: "I can do this. I always finish strong. I'm going to finish this drill. This is easy. I always win. I can do hard things, because I am a champion."

The cool thing about this exercise is that you can practice it any time, any place, any circumstance, with anybody. It won't take long for the mind to accept this new information as reality. In the process, you are reprogramming the powerful subconscious mind to work for you on your behalf. The brain doesn't judge, it simply takes the information (in this case, thoughts and inner dialogue) and creates new pathways and neural connections. In time, you will have created new habits for success, and your self-talk will be positive and self-affirming with little effort. Great athletes master this process, and you can too.

"Tackle the Dream Killers Campaign"

At the conclusion of this project, you will launch your Protect the Dream Club at your school. Choose a social-media platform and create a POPP Club group page. Now begin working on your group project that will be featured at our "41st Day Celebration." Some teams choose a rap or spoken word, others make a short video, while others might do a live skit or make a music video. Express your commitment to become Protectors of the Dream on your campus. And remember our tagline: Hope Is the New Dope!

"Leaders aren't born, they are made. And they are made just like anything else, through hard work. And that's the price we'll have to pay to achieve that goal, or any goal."

—Vince Lombardi

For the second half of our Protect the Dream Campaign, we will turn our attention to leadership. Having worked on the inside over the past few weeks, now it's time to begin impacting those in your sphere of influence, in a positive way. Let's go outside and begin the workout.

SECOND HALF: LEADERSHIP

KAREEM ABDUL-JABBAR

"Fundamental preparation is always effective. Work on those parts of your game that are fundamentally weak."

"I think that the good and the great are only separated by the willingness to sacrifice."

—Kareem Abdul-Jabbar

Day Twenty-One

From My Perspective

I loved watching the "Showtime" Lakers of the eighties. They were run-and-gun, high-octane, high-entertainment basketball with Hollywood celebrities lining the court night in and night out. Magic Johnson led the way with his electrifying no-look passes, but it was Kareem Abdul-Jabbar who scored like no one else in NBA history. And it was one shot that set him apart from all the rest: his signature "sky hook." It was literally unstoppable. You couldn't block it, or even get near it. It was a thing of beauty, and he rode it all the way to becoming the all-time NBA scoring leader. He could have done it the way every other big man always had, but instead he created something unique, something never seen before. You could do that. Use your imagination, then get to work. Find a part of your game that is still hidden—that thing that will set you apart.

Fascinating Facts

Kareem Abdul-Jabbar is a six-time NBA Champion, six-time NBA Most Valuable Player, and nineteen-time All Star. Playing in Los Angeles for the "Showtime" Lakers led Kareem into show business in Hollywood. He made his acting debut in Bruce Lee's film *Game of Death* in 1972. Then, in 1980, he played copilot Roger Murdock in the comedy hit *Airplane!*[22] Sports can open many doors for you if you learn the valuable life lessons along the way.

Today's Achievements

---

[22] Harlem World Magazine, "Harlem's Kareem Abdul-Jabbar," *Harlem World*, April 19, 2015, http://harlemworldmag.com/harlems-kareem-abdul-jabbar-1947/.

Today I want you to identify a teammate who is struggling to be their best. Challenge them in an inspiring way to push themselves. Convince them that the team needs them in order to be champions. Use your influence as a leader to motivate players on your team to realize their true potential. You're built for this.

"To me it was never about what I accomplished on the football field, it was about the way I played the game."

"I went out there to play my game for the fun of it and never based my career around records."

—Jerry Rice

Day Twenty-Two

From My Perspective

I watched as the 49ers dominated the NFL in the late eighties and early nineties, and Jerry Rice was one of the main reasons. While not the biggest, strongest, or fastest of players, he more than made up for it with his flawless technique. His training regimen in the off-season was truly legendary. He was the epitome of consistency, discipline, and work ethic. After achieving ultimate success, he could have rested on his laurels, but he didn't. He continued pushing himself as if he were competing not against other athletes, but himself. Have you ever asked yourself just how good you could be? That is, if you really pushed yourself to the limit perfect repetition and consistent training will program your subconscious mind to perform on your behalf so you can be laser-focused and concentrate consciously in the moment. Train like a champion today.

Fascinating Facts

Jerry Rice went to the Pro Bowl thirteen times; he was the NFL's Most Valuable Player in 1987, and a three-time Super Bowl Champion. Rice was one of eight children, and learned his incredible work ethic from his father, a hardworking bricklayer. Spending grueling hours as an assistant to his father in the sweltering Mississippi heat, it is said that Jerry learned his hand-eye coordination by catching bricks thrown at him by his father! [23] Are you building the character and discipline now that will serve you later in life? The great ones did.

Today's Achievements

[23] Biography.com, s.v. "Jerry Rice," updated April 1, 2014, https://www.biography.com/people/jerry-rice-40545.

Today I want you to strive to capture every thought and make it obedient to your vision of what you truly desire. Winning the mental battle on a regular basis, until it is engrained as a habit, is crucial to victory. Remember, success is primarily mental. Many athletes have raw talent, just as you do, but do not necessarily excel in their sport. Pay attention to that little voice in your head. You have the tools athletically. If you can learn to control your most valuable resource (your brain), then there will be little in this world that you cannot accomplish.

TODAY'S ACTION-CHALLENGE

"Concentration comes out of a combination of confidence and hunger."

"I've always made a total effort, even when the odds seemed entirely against me. I never quit trying; I never felt that I didn't have a chance to win."

—Arnold Palmer

Day Twenty-Three

From My Perspective

Golf has always been a gentlemen's game with polite and respectful crowds—all about etiquette—and then came "Arnie's Army." I would have loved to have seen Arnold Palmer battle Jack Nicklaus in the sixties, as a brand-new kind of golf fan had emerged: hardworking, blue-collar, regular folks. And Arnold was their hero. He was bold and aggressive, with an untraditional swing and a flare for the dramatic. He forever changed the game, as he brought something that had never been seen before. Nowadays young golfers pump their fists, show their passion, and play to the crowds. They wouldn't be there without Mr. Palmer. Could you inspire your team with a whole new energy? Energy and enthusiasm spring from passion, and passion flows from purpose. Remember why you play the game, and play with enthusiasm today.

Fascinating Facts

Arnold Palmer is generally regarded as one of the greatest golfers of all time. He won sixty-two PGA events and seven major titles. He won the PGA Tour Lifetime Achievement Award in 1998, and was one of the thirteen original inductees into the World Golf Hall of Fame. Palmer was nicknamed "The King" and was one of the first superstars of the sports-television age, which began in the

1950s. Before there were superstar athletes with record-setting contracts and huge endorsement deals, there was Arnie. Crowds followed him and loved him, as he brought a fresh, new enthusiasm to his sport and changed the game of golf forever. His loyal fans got a nickname as well: "Arnie's Army." It is said that soldiers from a nearby base attended the 1958 Masters holding homemade signs to show their support. The name "Arnie's Army" stuck, and he would be a hero to common folks for the rest of his stellar career. You could inspire people as well. Learn to use the gifts you have been given to inspire others. You'll be amazed what you can accomplish if you push yourself beyond your self-imposed limits.

Today's Achievements

Today let's focus on the information you let into your conscious mind. I want you to use YouTube and invest just a few minutes to feed your competitive spirit. Search "inspirational videos" and choose one or two short, powerful clips that will change your energy and focus your mind. If you make this a daily habit, you will set yourself apart from your competition and program your subconscious mind to help you achieve your goals and dreams. Invest in YOURSELF today.

TODAY'S ACTION-CHALLENGE

"Luck has nothing to do with it, because I have spent many, many hours, countless hours, on the court working for my one moment in time, not knowing when it would come."

"If you can keep playing tennis when somebody is shooting a gun down the street, that's concentration."

—Serena Williams

Day Twenty-Four

From My Perspective

Watching Serena Williams play "mere mortals" is just not fair. Power, speed, agility, and a fierce competitive spirit. She could have been another tough kid coming out of Compton, but she rose above. With the help of their father, who is their coach, Serena and Venus Williams have dominated women's tennis for decades—and they opened the door for girls who never would have considered tennis. Where would Serena be without the guidance, support, and accountability of a coach who cared? You have people in your life like that. I hope you appreciate them today. One day you'll look back and realize that these are the good ole days, and your coaches will become some of the greatest characters in your life story. Value them.

Fascinating Facts

Serena Williams holds thirty-nine major tennis titles (which is the most all-time among active players), twenty-three singles titles, fourteen doubles titles, and two mixed-doubles titles. She and her sister, Venus, have dominated the women's circuit for decades. With her father as her coach, Serena began playing at the age of five on public courts in Compton, known at the time as South Central LA. Her skills developed rapidly, and sports were her way out of a tough neighborhood dominated by Crips and Bloods.

Children playing sports in Compton in the mideighties competed to the sound of gunfire in the background.[24] What obstacles do you face today in your training and workouts? Adversity made Serena tough—it can do the same for you.

Today's Achievements

[24] Edmondson, Jacqueline. *Venus and Serena Williams: A Biography.* Westport, CT: Greenwood Press, 2005.

By now you're over halfway to your goal of successfully completing your 40 Days of Power project. Hopefully you have been reviewing your goals daily, but today I want you to take a close look at what you are working to accomplish. It's time to check in and acknowledge your progress, but also see if your goals are stretching you. If need be, increase them and keep pushing yourself. What you focus on expands, so continue to monitor your dreams and keep them in front you. Keep chasing your dreams—that's what the great ones do.

TODAY'S ACTION-CHALLENGE

WEEKLY HUDDLE

Week-Four Dream Killer: Unhealthy Relationships

At your age, who you choose to be in your peer group could not be more crucial as to who you will become. It has been said that we are the collective average of the five people we spend the most time with. This is a principle of energy. Our energy begins to flow and vibrate at the speed and frequency of those we "move" with. You can't get around this phenomenon. Who you let into your unique little world will powerfully affect your perspective and how you think, talk, act, and feel. Look at your life goals and dreams again. Ask yourself if the people closest to you truly care about what you want and where you want to go in life. Choose deliberately and wisely, and be honest. I promise you, one day you really will care.

Discussion Questions

1) Think of your best friends. How did they come to be in your inner circle? No judgment, just honest assessment of your current squad.

2) Look around this group and choose someone you want to bring into your sphere of influence. Share with them what you value about them, and ask them to share one major turning point in their life that was brought about by a friendship.

3) Share your standards for what a best friend should be. How do they live around you, and how do they add to your life?

4) What are three things you can do as a team to make EVERY player on this team feel included?

Week-Four Power Grade: _____

Three Lessons Learned This Week:

O

O

O

WEEK-FOUR POPP EXERCISE
Winning team gets "Hope Is the New Dope" gear!

WEEK FIVE

I will not prejudge people, situations, or opportunities; I will observe and overcome.

When we prejudge our opponents by mere appearances, we often overlook their strengths or exaggerate their weaknesses, which only serves to weaken our game plan and give our rivals an advantage. None of us are good fortune-tellers, and there is no way to know the outcome of certain situations. So why would we assume we will lose just because we're down a certain number of points, or that we will be defeated by a supposedly superior opponent, or that we will blow a team out just by showing up? That's why we play the game. This book is filled with champions who defied the odds and made miraculous comebacks, many of whom were once underdogs before they were superstars. Stay in the moment and take on each challenge as it comes. Observe, adjust, and overcome.

POPP Power Principle #5
Thoughts Become Things, and Words Create Our World.

Momentum is a mysterious force that can affect the entire outcome of a contest. It has nothing to do with superstition, and everything to do with confidence or lack thereof. One play alone cannot create or reverse momentum, but rather a team's response to that play, or series of plays, can make all the difference. An interception, a steal, a blocked punt, a costly penalty, a slam dunk, a home run . . . These plays alone won't necessarily cost you the game, but if they create chaos, confusion, or disunity, then they can sink your ship. Games are often decided by a team's response or reaction to these emotionally charged energy swings, and often the crowd's enthusiasm also plays a role. Can a player manage the space between his or her ears when the game seems to be slipping away? Or when you're way ahead and need to maintain focus? At these crucial times, thoughts and words are everything. If there's a sack at a crucial point in a potential game-winning drive, what if your team gets the "Oh no, here we go again" mind virus? At these times, repetition is either your enemy or your friend; what you have practiced will take over. Leaders must step up and have the language and mindset of a champion, and snatch the momentum back. But that doesn't just happen, especially under pressure—it is developed over hours of training and creating powerful habits and pathways in simulated situations. One play at a time, the player who can control their emotions, discipline their minds, and communicate their confidence to the team in the midst of a firestorm will typically prevail. The right thoughts, and the right words, carefully chosen and repeated, can bring power back onto your side of the field.

CAUTION FLAG

Pay attention to all the drug references you hear and see this week: in your music, movies, video games, and social media. Simply notice, that is the first step.

Watch Week-Five POPP Video

This week we will get into the minds of those who have achieved what few others ever have. This week: **NO PREJUDICE**. Reclaim your power.

Coaches Corner

Knute Rockne[25]

Knute Rockne coached during an era when it was a given that athletes played through pain and even serious injury, while making so little that players needed full-time jobs in the off-season to support their families. Can you imagine what practices were like for these warriors before all the cameras, social media, political correctness, and lawsuits—these were real men preparing for real battle—may the best man win. I miss watching sports from that era, when it was about pride and bragging rights, rather than stats and paychecks. Now, I'm not saying that today's athletes aren't warriors; many are fine-tuned machines. But unfortunately,

---

[25] Steele, Michael R. *Knute Rockne: A Portrait of a Notre Dame Legend.* New York: Sports Publishing, 1999.

as skill, technology, and science have advanced, healthy attitudes and mutual respect for your opponent have eroded and declined. This week when your coaches push you beyond your imaginary limits, remember these honorable men of old who relied on heart and toughness rather than fancy equipment and social media. May the best man win.

Achievements

Knute Rockne led Notre Dame to National Championship titles in 1924, 1929, and 1930. Rockne's 1924 team went undefeated and featured the legendary "Four Horsemen" backfield of football stars. The Coach tragically died in a plane crash in a cornfield in Kansas in 1931, and it shocked the nation. The outpouring of love and support culminated with the hit Hollywood film, Knute Rockne, All American. The film starred Ronald Reagan in the supporting role portraying running back George Gip, who died in 1920 at the end of his senior season. The movie features the famous scene when Rockne inspires his team at halftime by encouraging them to "Win one for the Gipper." Are you an inspiration to your teammates?

"Play like you're positive on the victory, even though they're leading big now."

"At home we're the hosts, and I never liked the idea of being embarrassed in front of our friends. On the road we're somebody else's guests, and we play in a way that they're not going to forget we visited them."

—Knute Rockne

Week-Five Local Flavor

Coach Al Morrell
Fellowship Christian Paladins
Roswell, GA

Al Morrell has been coaching for over thirty-five years. In his distinguished career, Coach Morrell helped Marietta High School post a perfect 40-0 record from 1989 to 1992; he was named Cherokee County Head Coach of the Year in 2012; he was inducted into the Cherokee County Gridiron Hall of Fame in 2013; and Morrell was named *Atlanta Journal-*

Constitution's Private School Class A Coach of the Year and Region 6A Coach of the Year in 2016.

Coach's Quote

"My philosophy is to show the kids that you care for them, love them, and want them to succeed. That's the greatest motivator for a coach. Wins and losses are important to me, but I value relationships most as a coach. The guys I have coached with are my best friends in life. Football is such a unique sport. You must have a strong work ethic as a coach and a player. As coaches, we have to share that message with the kids."

—Al Morrell

"It kills me to lose. If I'm a troublemaker, and I don't think that my temper makes me one, then it's because I can't stand losing. That's the way I am about winning. All I ever wanted to do was finish first."

"Many people resented my impatience and honesty, but I never cared about acceptance as much as I cared about respect."

—Jackie Robinson

Day Twenty-Five

From My Perspective

Jackie Robinson struck fear into pitchers, fielders, and catchers. As soon as he got on base, the crowd got excited and the other team got nervous. He single-handedly changed the game forever with his legs. But what inspires me even more was the way he continued to compete at the highest level while facing hatred, bigotry, racism, and vitriol at every stadium he visited and from the majority of fans and opposing players he faced. He rose above the threats, curses, rocks and bottles, and ugliness to impact the game so much that ALL of Major League Baseball retired his number forty-two forever. What is the toughest obstacle you are facing today? Rise above and make a statement with your game, rather than your mouth.

Fascinating Facts

Jackie Robinson was a six-time MLB All Star, National League MVP, NL Batting Champion, and 1955 World Series Champion. Robinson faced racial abuse, jeers, slurs, and even death threats throughout his career after entering the minor leagues as the first black player. Some opponents even went so far as to cancel exhibition games just to keep him from playing. Even some of his own teammates turned on him and signed a petition to try to keep him off the team, and pitcher Kirby Higbe refused to play with Robinson and was eventually traded because of it. However, some of his teammates, and eventually the league as a whole, finally accepted Jackie. In a famous demonstration of solidarity, during one game, teammate Pee Wee Reese put his arm around Robinson in front of the crowd, and Pittsburg Pirate player Hank Greenberg (a Jewish ball player who had endured some of the same treatment) encouraged Jackie when the two met on the field.[26] Robinson broke the color barrier in professional sports at a time in our nation's history when most thought it was impossible to do so. It is always impossible until someone does it. Will you take a stand at your school for kids who are left out, ridiculed, and mistreated? Jackie did, and so can you.

Today's Achievements

---

[26] Evan Andrews, "11 Things You May Not Know about Jackie Robinson," History.com, January 31, 2014, http://www.history.com/news/11-things-you-may-not-know-about-jackie-robinson.

You are the collective average of the five people you spend the most time with. Today I want you to identify who your inner circle is, and take an honest look at the impact they are making on your life. Are they 100 percent supportive of your goals and dreams? Are any of them getting in the way of what you truly desire? You must be VERY selective of who you let into your inner squad. You can love them, but also protect your dream if they are not helping you achieve it. Choose wisely; you'll care one day.

"It's like all guys want to do is make a dunk, grab their shirt, and yell out and scream—they could be down thirty points but that's what they do. Okay, so you made a dunk. Get back down the floor on defense!"

"When you play against different people from all walks of life, you can't do the same thing against every player defensively or offensively. You have to change up the way you go at a player."

—Oscar Robertson

Day Twenty-Six

From My Perspective

Before they even called it a triple-double, the "Big O" averaged one for an entire season. Double-digit averages in points, rebounds, and assists—a feat that would not be equaled for another fifty-five years. Before there were Magic and Michael, there was Oscar Robertson. He invented the moves we now take for granted. Many young players today who are signing eight-figure contracts owe their careers to trailblazers like Oscar. There are still moves that have yet to be created, techniques to be invented, and unique gifts to be unveiled. But these innovations are discovered when no one is watching, during the countless hours working on your craft. They say it takes ten thousand hours of practice to become a master. Now, I don't know if that is true, but it does mean it's time to get to work.

Fascinating Facts

Oscar Robertson was an NBA Most Valuable Player, twelve-time NBA All Star, and 1971 NBA Champion. Oscar grew up very poor, and he and his family lived in the ghetto in Indianapolis. He was introduced to basketball by his brothers, who played at the local YMCA. His brother Bailey even went on to play with the Harlem Globetrotters![27] As you can see, many of these legendary athletes came from little, but rose above to achieve greatness. Can you rise above your current struggles in order to find the champion within?

<u>Today's Achievements</u>

---

[27] Indiana Basketball Hall of Fame. "Bailey Robertson." Indiana Basketball Hall of Fame. Accessed September 18, 2017.
http://www.hoopshall.com/hall-of-fame/bailey-robertson/.

Today let's analyze how your practices and workouts are really going during this project. Be honest with yourself about your overall effort. Set your sincere goal today to have the most intense, focused, and relentless training you have experienced thus far. Keep in mind that all your other teammates are getting this same challenge today, so it should be ultracompetitive on the field or court. Get after it.

"Back before I injured my hip, I thought going to the gym was for wimps."

"Set your goals high, and don't stop till you get there."

—Bo Jackson

Day Twenty-Seven

From My Perspective

I had the pleasure of watching Bo Jackson's entire career: running all over the SEC while at Auburn, running over linebackers in the NFL, and literally running up the outfield walls in Major League Baseball. He did everything well—raw, God-given talent. However, as a kid he was well on his way to getting into real trouble before sports saved him. Maybe you're a little like Bo. God reached down and gave you a special gift at birth, but perhaps He also gave you a strong will and possibly a rebellious spirit. Sports could be your saving grace as well. Apply yourself today. Do it because you're grateful; do it because you want a strong character; do it because somebody believes in you. Just do it.

Fascinating Facts

Bo Jackson won the Heisman Trophy in 1985, was an MLB All Star in 1989, and made the NFL Pro Bowl in 1990—becoming the only player to be an All Star in professional baseball AND football. Because of his success in multiple sports, Bo starred in one of the most popular sports ad campaigns of 1989–1990. The "Bo Knows" campaign envisioned Jackson taking up a variety of different sports including tennis, golf, luge, auto racing, and even playing blues music with Bo Diddley, who scolded Jackson by telling him, "You don't know Diddley!"[28] Bo Jackson's God-given natural ability vaulted him to a status few athletes ever achieve. Has God given you a rare gift? Give it away, in order to keep it.

Today's Achievements

---

[28] Nike. "Bo Knows." Television advertisement. Wieden+Kennedy, directed by Joe Pytka, 1989.

The quality of your life depends on the quality of your questions. Today I want you to sincerely ask your coach and a parent or teacher what he or she thinks about your attitude, effort, and leadership during this campaign. Ask them to be brutally honest, and receive their response and input. I want you to want to know, so you can accurately assess your progress. Your mentors see your life every day, and they will shoot straight with you. Regardless of their answer, make it your firm conviction to set your standards even higher. That's why we compete—to get better and better and to reach higher and higher.

TODAY'S ACTION-CHALLENGE

MARIO ANDRETTI

"If everything seems under control, you're just not going fast enough."

"If you're so afraid of failure, you will never succeed. You have to take chances."

—Mario Andretti

Day Twenty-Eight

From My Perspective

It's hard to imagine competing in a sport where every time you suit up, it could literally cost you your life. Racing around winding tracks against other adrenaline junkies, traveling at speeds of up to 225 mph, Mario Andretti's rivals were watching his back and trying to catch him—and seeing him in the winner's circle once again. Something deep inside drove him to be the best and the fastest. Nobody had to tell him to go fast he just flew. How fast could you go in your life if you removed all your fear? Fear is a paper tiger, an impotent bully. Face your fear, and overcome it. At the end of the day, the one you're really competing against is YOU. Go fast—you were built for it.

Fascinating Facts

Mario Andretti is one of the most successful racing drivers of all time. He is one of only two drivers in history to have won races in Formula One, IndyCar, World Sportscar Championship, and NASCAR (as well as winning races in midget cars and sprint cars!). Andretti also won the highly coveted Indianapolis 500, Daytona 500, and Formula One World Championship. Mario found the "Winners Circle"an incredible 109 times on major circuits, and no American has won a Formula One race since Andretti's victory at the 1978 Dutch Grand Prix. The Andretti's family lived in Croatia until 1948, when they fled to a refugee camp in Italy. They later immigrated to the United States in 1955, and Andretti became a US citizen in 1964.[29] Adversity can make you into a champion too, if you let it.

Today's Achievements

---

[29] ESPN. "Mario Andretti." ESPN.co.uk. Accessed September 18, 2017. http://en.espn.co.uk/alfaromeo/motorsport/driver/911.html.

Today let's focus on one of the most important questions you can ask: WHY? Take a fresh look at your goals-and-dreams list from the beginning of this forty-day project. You have already determined WHAT you want, and your coaches are helping you with the HOW. But why do you want what you say you want? We are attempting with this program to give you the tools to become positive role models in your school and community. But if you don't have a BIG WHY behind what you want, then your plans will lack passion and power. Ask the right questions, and you will discover the right answers to help you become who you wish to be.

TODAY'S ACTION-CHALLENGE

ROBERTO CLEMENTE

"If you have a chance to accomplish something that will make things better for people coming behind you, and you don't do that, you are wasting your time on this earth."

"I am convinced that God wanted me to be a baseball player."

—Roberto Clemente

Day Twenty-Nine

From My Perspective

Roberto Clemente was an outstanding baseball player; nobody questions that. But remarkably, he was an even better human being. He used his success in professional sports to help those less fortunate, especially children. In today's age of spoiled, overpaid superstars and scandals, Clemente is a light that still shines bright. We need more athletes who give back to their communities for all they've been given. This is the heart of this program—to use your influence as an athlete at your school and make it a better place—a better place for weaker kids, a better place for the bullied, a better place for kids who just don't fit in. You have no idea how much a little attention from a player like you could do for a student who is losing hope. Use your influence for peace, and if you think you don't have that much influence, then get to work and do something about that.

Fascinating Facts

Roberto Clemente was a two-time World Series Champion, a fifteen-time MLB All Star, and National League MVP. Clemente joined the rare "3000 Hit Club" getting the three thousandth hit of his storied career on his LAST at-bat! His life was tragically cut short during a flight from his native Puerto Rico to Nicaragua delivering aid packages to earthquake victims.[30] He gave his life serving less-fortunate ones, which is an even greater legacy than the one he left on the baseball diamond. What will your lasting legacy be?

Today's Achievements

---

[30] Tim Karan, "21 Facts You May Not Know about Roberto Clemente on the Anniversary of His Debut," Bleacher Report, April 17, 2012, http://bleacherreport.com/articles/1149087-21-facts-you-may-not-know-about-roberto-clemente-on-the-anniversary-of-his-debut.

Great athletes have synchronized their mind, body, and spirit. When standout players get into that elusive "zone," it is because they have found a way to get all three of those areas aligned and working. Oftentimes the area that gets neglected is your spiritual side. Today take a few minutes and pray to the God of your understanding. Ask Him to help you be the best person you can possibly be, and have a powerful positive impact in your school and community. Better yet, ask your POPP Power Partner to join you in this challenge. Can you imagine what would happen if your team started pulling together in all three of these areas? Go deep all the answers you seek are inside of you.

"If you want to be the best, you have to do things that other people aren't willing to do."

"I want to be able to look back and say, 'I've done everything I can, and I was successful.' I don't want to look back and say I should have done this or that."

—Michael Phelps

Day Thirty

From My Perspective

I was on the swim team as a kid . . . for one day. Then I self-discovered my way out of the pool. (It's a lot harder than it looks!) Ever since then I have had respect for those who can swim fast and swim for a long time. It is said that Michael Phelps trained four-to-six hours a day, every day, for four years—without a single day off (even if that is urban legend, we know he trained like a BEAST!). No days off for illness, no days off for vacation, no days off for holidays, no days off for rest, no days off. Period. He was laser focused on his goal: to be the greatest swimmer to have ever lived. And he did even better than that: he is now, by far, the most decorated Olympic athlete in history. Do you think he regrets training so hard? After winning a record eight gold medals at the Beijing Games in 2008, he found some much publicized trouble. However, he rebounded and came back to win four golds in 2012, and five more in 2016. A champion falls seven times, but rises again. Keep your focus and rely on your teammates. Trouble finds you when you are being lazy and unfocused, with nothing much to do. You're better than that. So let's get busy—again.

Fascinating Facts

Michael Phelps is a swimmer and the most decorated Olympian of all time, with an unbelievable total of twenty-eight medals (twenty-three of them gold!). Phelps won eight gold medals at the Beijing Games in 2008, breaking fellow American swimmer Mark Spitz's record of seven golds at the Munich Games in 1972. He was the most successful athlete of the games for four straight Olympics—an amazing accomplishment. Phelps was born to swim: six feet four inches tall, a seventy-nine-inch arm span, the torso of a six-foot-eight man, unusually short legs for his height, oversized hands and feet, AND he happens to be double jointed, which allows him to whip his arms, legs, and feet with a greater range of motion than most of his competitors.[31] Some would say he is the winner of the genetic lottery! What if he hadn't found the swimming pool? But he did, by following his passion. How can sports change your life? You'll never know until you push yourself beyond your limits.

Today's Achievements

---

[31] Staff Reporter, "How Michael Phelps' Body Was Made for Swimming, and Why He Could Slack Off and Still Win," International Science Times, August 5, 2012,
http://www.isciencetimes.com/articles/3593/20120805/michael-phelps-body-made-swimming-why-slack.htm.

Today I want you to honestly identify the one area of your life that is the biggest obstacle to your goals and dreams. It could be an unhealthy relationship, a destructive habit, laziness or procrastination, trouble at home, or struggles with your grades. Whatever it is, you need to bring a trusted friend into your battle. Share this weakness with your Power Partner or a coach, and get some help. Two are better than one, and you have people in your life who care.

TODAY'S ACTION-CHALLENGE

Week-Five Dream Killer: Disrespecting Authorities

In many other world cultures, the wise and "elders" are held in the highest regard and treated with utmost respect. Today in America we are dealing with an identity crisis among our young people. Many have no idea who they really are and are missing out on one of the most valuable resources they possess: the elders in their lives. Coaches, teachers, parents, and preachers; judges, officers, grandparents, and those who are older and wiser who come into your life. These people have been around the sun more times than you and have acquired a wealth of wisdom, knowledge, and experience that you would be wise to pay attention to. Regardless of how you feel about them as individuals, it is never appropriate or wise to disrespect authority figures. Just think of all the young people you know who live their lives with no respect for authority—things rarely if ever end well for them, because it goes against the natural order of things, and it will eventually catch up with you.

Discussion Questions

1) Identify and name the authority figures in your life.

2) Define the word RESPECT. Discuss what respect looks like. Share specific times when you have witnessed disrespect of authorities at your school.

3) Think of the last time you disrespected an authority. Share how you can make it right,

and how you can treat that person respectfully in the future.

4) Discuss how disrespect has shipwrecked the dreams of someone you know. (Don't mention specific names; that wouldn't be respectful to them.) What are three things you can do as a team to increase the overall level of respect for the authority figures at your school?

Week-Five Power Grade: _____

Three Lessons Learned This Week:

O

O

O

WEEK-FIVE POPP EXERCISE
Winning team gets "Hope Is the New Dope" gear!

WEEK SIX

*When wrong, I will promptly admit it
and quickly make amends.*

The battle is mental, before it ever gets played out on the court or the field. Mistakes are not fatal and failures are not final, unless of course you continue to make the same ones over and over, or if you can't move past them quickly. Games are won by minimizing mistakes and executing game plans. Problems arise when we screw up and then let it affect team chemistry. When the blame game begins and excuses take over, then the momentum shifts to the other side of the field. Control that which you can control. Quickly take responsibility, and get your head back in the game. It makes a big difference when a teammate owns the play and resets. It is contagious and can quickly redirect the energy.

POPP Power Principle #6
Passion and Drive are Found in My Unique Gift.

Extraordinary athletes bring their mind, body, and spirit into alignment and get into that illusory place many refer to as "the zone." When a player is in the zone, everything slows down and you can see things almost before they seem to happen. Huge openings appear before you, the basket seems bigger, the baseball seems to be the size of a grapefruit, and you feel stronger, faster, and more agile. What's the quickest way to exit the zone? Make a stupid mistake or commit a foolish foul; a turnover, a penalty, or a careless error can shake your confidence and knock you right out of your groove. This is when we need to access our power and move back into the flow. The truly great ones have the ability to move into the Power Zone when the stakes are highest and when their team needs them the most. It's all about finding your passion and will, and those things spring from purpose.

We were all gifted with God-given talents when we came into this world. The key is figuring out what you love and what makes you come alive; do that, and you are one of the lucky ones. The legendary athletes found in this book figured it out. It's as if they were born to play their sport, and they somehow instinctively knew it. To excel, you must LOVE the game. Figure out your God-given gift and give it wholeheartedly. Play for the love of the game and don't take yourself too seriously. Mistakes are just mistakes. Shake it off and don't make the fatal mistake: being taken totally out of your game because you lose your head. When the game is on the line, tap into your unique gift and enjoy the moment, and simply love the game. You were born for it.

CAUTION FLAG

Pay attention to students this week who get little attention. Just notice them, and remind yourself that they have a unique story. Awareness is the first step.

Watch Week-Six POPP Video

This week we will get into the minds of those who have achieved what few others ever have. This week: **MAKE AMENDS**. Reclaim your power.

Coaches Corner

John Wooden[32]

I've never heard anyone say anything negative about John Wooden—literally. I'm sure it has happened, just never to me. Imagine a life so well lived that no one had anything bad to say about you. And he could have been easy to hate, because his teams dominated and everyone was out to beat him. During the sixties, all he did was win championships. But all these years later, what he is remembered for is his wisdom, spirituality, and character. As a matter of fact, many character and leadership programs are based on his timeless doctrines and spiritual teachings. He coached and raised up some of the greatest players the NBA has ever seen. One day you will also be remembered more for your character and integrity than for your athletic ability and popularity, although that is hard to

---

[32] Wooden, John. *They Call Me Coach.* New York: McGraw-Hill Education, 2004.

imagine when you are young. This week, make decisions you will be proud of when you are a father or a mother, or a grandparent for that matter.

Achievements

John Wooden was one of the brightest minds in basketball history. He directed his UCLA men's basketball teams to an unbelievable ten NCAA National Championships in twelve years. He coached many former stars, including Kareem-Abdul Jabbar, Bill Walton, and Gail Goodrich. During his brilliant forty-year career, he had a winning percentage of .813. On one of his many streaks, his Bruins won eighty-eight games straight, and during another, he won thirty-eight consecutive NCAA tournament games—that is complete domination. Coach Wooden was named College Basketball Coach of the Year six times, and he was the first to be elected into the Naismith Memorial Basketball Hall of Fame as a coach AND a player. Are you currently on a winning streak? All it takes is one play.

"Be more concerned with your character than your reputation, because your character is what you really are, while your reputation is merely what others think you are."

"Don't measure yourself by what you have accomplished, but by what you should have accomplished with your ability."

—John Wooden

Week-Six Local Flavor

To begin this week, I would like to feature my high school basketball coach, Larry Pace. I grew up on the west side of Cobb County, and that side of town was all I'd ever known. But when George Walton Comprehensive High School was built, my parents moved the family to East Cobb in the summer of 1978. I didn't know anyone, except for my best friend, Scott, and I didn't come from where these kids came from (this was a much more affluent area). But I was a two-sport athlete, and I was able to fit in rather quickly. One reason was because of the teachers and coaches in my life who took an interest in me. Coach Larry Pace and I have stayed connected for thirty-five years since I graduated in 1982. I admire and respect him greatly, and he had a profound impact on my life. You'll be amazed how long the things these men and women have taught you will stay with you throughout your life—it would do you good to pay attention.

Coach Larry Pace
Walton Raiders
Marietta, GA

Coach Larry Pace retired in 2010 after forty-two years serving his community as a high school teacher. He left coaching to become a better husband and dad to his wife and two sons, and he became the activities director for the youth at his church. Coach Pace began teaching and coaching basketball at the junior-high level in Cobb County schools, where he won two Boys Championships. Pace was the first varsity boys basketball and baseball coach at Walton High School in East Marietta. He coached basketball for fifteen years with two subregion championships.

Coach's Quote

"I always strived to teach and coach in line with my personality, true to myself, and with a strong emphasis on fundamentals. At all levels, I believe in developing the teamwork attitude to win, and to achieve greater success for ALL the players on the team. I want to leave with you a lifelong lesson that I teach: don't turn over your faith in the game of life."

—Larry Pace

"I love it when people doubt me. It makes me work harder to prove them wrong."

"There may be people who have more talent than you, but there's no excuse for anyone to work harder than you do—and I believe that."

—Derek Jeter

Day Thirty-One

From My Perspective

I grew up in the South, and to be quite honest, I don't like the Yankees. In 1996, up two games to none, the Yankees came back and beat my Braves in the best-of-seven World Series. It would have been back-to-back titles for the Braves, as it looked like we were on our way to building our own dynasty—but it wasn't meant to be. Although I tried, I just couldn't hate Derek Jeter. He played the game right: He stayed out of trouble, he stayed out of the tabloids, he made plays, he controlled his temper, and he respected the game. And he was the most dangerous when the game was on the line. He loved to have the game on his shoulders, with two on and two out in the bottom of the ninth, against the other team's best closer, with all the pressure and the bright, hot spotlight directly on him . . . and it seemed he always got the big hit and broke the other team's heart. I wish we had more players like him today. Can you play the game with respect? Can you handle the spotlight? It takes character to do that, and it is not given—you have to earn it. Others have gone before you and paved the way so you could play the game you love. Honor them, and play the game right.

Fascinating Facts

Derek Jeter is a five-time World Series Champion, a fourteen-time MLB All Star, and the 2000 World Series MVP. Jeter's parents both served in the US military, and they instilled

189

structure and discipline in him from an early age. When Derek was a child, his parents had him sign a contract every year that held him to certain standards of acceptable behavior. They also taught him to be a positive person by insisting he never use the word "can't."[33] Your parents or guardians have molded you into the person you are today, one way or another. Are you grateful for the ones who have shaped your life? Show them today.

Today's Achievements

---

[33] Howard, Johnette. July 8, 2011. "Don't forget what got Derek Jeter here." ESPN.com. Accessed September 18, 2017. http://www.espn.com/new-york/mlb/columns/story?columnist=howard_johnette&id=6742913.

Today I want you to practice "lifting up" your teammates, because that's what true leaders do. Pay attention to the attitude, effort, and drive of the other participants in this program. Communicate what you see to them. If they inspire you, tell them and thank them. If they are slacking, then challenge them to get their head back in the game. If they are discouraged or down, then inspire them with words of affirmation and convince them that you believe in them. Team unity is crucial, and you can be the catalyst that brings your squad together.

ROGER FEDERER

"What I think I've been able to do well over the years is play with pain, play with problems, play in all sorts of conditions."

"I've always been aware that the image you patiently construct for an entire career can be ruined in a minute. It scares you a bit, but that's the way things are."

—Roger Federer

Day Thirty-Two

From My Perspective

I never played much tennis myself, but I was good friends with several All-American tennis players who were part of the University of Georgia NCAA Championship teams of the early eighties. I witnessed through my friends what it took to be a champion in that sport. They had to say no to many of the things that seemingly everyone else in Athens was saying yes to. Passion will do that—teach you to say NO. Roger Federer has accomplished what no other male has ever done in the world of tennis, winning eighteen Grand Slam titles. Most players dream of winning just one Grand Slam, as that sets you apart and you are in the history books forever. He did it year after year, and he did it with class. A gentleman—calm, cool, and collected, unflappable. When the pressure was on, he never lost his cool. When he was defeated, though it was rare, it only drove him even harder to come back and win another championship. Here's a challenge for you: Pick ONE thing in your life, and make a firm decision that you are going to do everything in your power to be the best at that one thing. What have you got to lose? Just some future regrets.

Fascinating Facts

Roger Federer has been called by many the greatest tennis player of all time. He is one of only eight men to have captured a Career Grand Slam (winning at least one of all four Grand Slam events). He has won nineteen Grand Slam singles titles, which is the most all time for male players, and he held the number-one spot in the ATP rankings for an astounding total of 302 weeks! That is complete domination. Interestingly, Roger grew up in Switzerland in an area close to both the German and French borders, so he speaks perfect German, French, and English. I would say that qualifies as a stand-out student athlete![34] Do you have what it takes to excel on the field AND in the classroom? Push yourself.

Today's Achievements

---

[34] Stauffer, Rene. *The Roger Federer Story: Quest for Perfection.* Chicago, IL: New Chapter Press, 2007.

Today it's time to ask another revealing question. Your family tends to know you at the deepest level. They see you at your best and your worst, when you are struggling and when you are thriving, when you are behaving and when you aren't. So why not ask them honestly what they see? Ask them if they have seen a difference in you over the last month, and ask them to be truthful. "What could I do better?" Truly listen and try not to resist or defend what they share. If they have seen a positive change in your attitude, then celebrate. If they haven't, then take it as a challenge to work harder and do better. Honest evaluation is what helps us grow. Go and get some intel from those who know you best.

"Winning doesn't always mean being first. Winning means you're doing better than you've ever done before."

"No matter what the competition is, I try to find a goal that day and better that goal."

—Bonnie Blair

Day Thirty-Three

From My Perspective

Imagine training for years: every day, every week, every month, with only one goal in mind—Olympic gold. All those countless hours of pain, injury, recovery, and more pain, in order to compete for just FORTY SECONDS. Talk about pressure. You have no room for error, no do-overs, no second chances. All you have is one shot, and less than a minute to make your mark on history. That's what Bonnie Blair did, and she did it better than anyone else who ever competed in her sport. Would you be willing to give that much of your life for something noble? Would you be willing to say no to all the distractions and temptations because your goal is more important to you? That's what champions do; they choose wisely, and invest in what is most important to them. You have 86,400 seconds today— invest them wisely.

Fascinating Facts

Bonnie Blair is a retired American speed skater. Bonnie is one of the most decorated athletes in Olympic history, and she was elected into the United States Olympic Hall of Fame in 2004. Blair represented the United States in four different Olympic Games, winning five gold medals and one bronze. While achieving ultra success in her sport, Bonnie also "gives back" in a very big way: She's a motivational speaker, she founded the Bonnie Blair Charitable Fund, and she supports the American Cancer Society and the Alzheimer's Association.[35] How can you give back to your community? Can you donate some of your time, talent, or treasure to those less fortunate? Always remember, givers get.

Today's Achievements

[35] Biography.com, s.v. "Bonnie Blair," last updated April 2, 2014, https://www.biography.com/people/bonnie-blair-9926791.

Make it your goal to make an outstanding play today—I mean a real game changer. Fly around the field, hustle down the court, attempt to stay ultra focused, and make the big play. Make it your goal to be THE impact player on the field today. First you must see it in your mind's eye, then go and find it in the game. Why not you, and why not now? (Keep in mind, your teammates have the same challenge today.)

"The ballplayer who loses his head, who can't keep his cool, is worse than no ballplayer at all."

"In the beginning I used to make one terrible play a game. Then I got so I'd make one a week and finally I'd pull a bad one about once a month. Now, I'm trying to keep it down to one a season."

—Lou Gehrig

Day Thirty-Four

From My Perspective

Unfortunately, many of this young generation only know Lou Gehrig's name because of the disease that took his life: ALS. I respect this great athlete as much for the way he died as I do for the way he lived. His nickname, "The Iron Horse," says so much about his strong will and indomitable spirit. On the day he stood in front of a packed house at Yankee Stadium to officially announce his retirement, he forever will be remembered for his tearful proclamation: "Today I consider myself the luckiest man on the face of the earth."[36] And this was said after he knew he would soon be dead. He died way too young at the age of thirty-seven. Today, remember that you are already building your legacy, even though you might be considered young. We are never promised another day, so live today like it is your last. You'll be amazed how fast it goes.

Fascinating Facts

Lou Gehrig was a seven-time MLB All Star, two-time American League MVP, and six-time World Series Champion, and he won the coveted Triple Crown Award in 1934. Gehrig played in 2,130 professional baseball games in a row—that is

---

[36] "Luckiest Man," Baseball Hall of Fame website, accessed August 22, 2017, http://baseballhall.org/discover/lou-gehrig-luckiest-man.

hard to fathom. It's even harder to believe when you consider the fact that he played through illnesses and injuries that included seventeen fractures in his hands and severe back pain. His consecutive-game record stood until 1995, when Cal Ripken Jr. finally broke it. In today's world of often-overpaid athletes who regularly miss considerable playing time on the injured-reserve list, the old-timers must be rolling over in their graves. Lou wouldn't have it that way. He loved to play the game.

Today's Achievements

Okay, we're heading down the home stretch now. Gut-check time. Respectfully ask your coach today if you can briefly address the team. Let the other players know the biggest change you have experienced over this forty-day project. Share with them why you are committed to this process and who you want to be for your teammates this season. Keep in mind everyone is getting this same challenge today, so make it your goal to be chosen to represent. Humbly let everyone see your progress— don't keep it to yourself.

"If we could have just screwed another head on his shoulders, he would have been the greatest golfer who ever lived."

"I couldn't wait for the sun to come up the next morning so that I could get out on the course again."

—Ben Hogan

Day Thirty-Five

From My Perspective

Obviously Ben Hogan played way before my time, but I wanted to include him because of his pursuit of excellence. Many attribute the mechanics of today's pure golf swing to this golfer. I wonder how many swings it took to perfect what many would say was the most beautiful golf swing in the history of the game. Players still try to imitate his swing, although he was refining it over seventy years ago. That is true and lasting impact. Are you willing to practice your skills, mechanics, and techniques over, and over, and over until you've mastered them? That's what the great ones do, and your rivals are out there practicing right now to beat you. Perfect practice makes perfect, and fundamentals really do matter. That's why your coaches make you do it again and again. Let's get it right.

Fascinating Facts

Ben Hogan is generally considered one of the greatest golfers in the history of the game. He won nine major championships, and he is one of only five players to have won all the major championships at least once. Hogan was a legendary ball striker and had a profound impact on swing theory, which is quite amazing considering the following. Hogan's career (and his life) was almost tragically cut short, at the age of thirty-six, on February 2,

1949. On a foggy bridge in Van Horn, Texas, early in the morning hours, Hogan and his wife, Valerie, and the Cadillac they were driving were struck head on by a Greyhound bus. With a double-fractured pelvis, a broken collarbone, a left-ankle fracture, a chipped rib, and near-fatal blood clots, Hogan was told he may never walk again, much less play competitive golf. Hogan had thrown himself across his wife to protect her right before the crash, and that most likely saved his life, as the steering column was hammered through the driver's seat. Incredibly, Hogan would go on to win the US Open less than a year later in 1950.[37] He would continue to dominate his sport in the following years, defying the odds. Will you rise above what people expect of you? Don't settle for less than you are capable of—reach higher.

Today's Achievements

---

[37] Hack, Damon. June 24, 2010. "Hogan's Return: Back From Tragedy to Win the 1950 U.S. Open." Golf.com. Accessed September 18, 2017. http://www.golf.com/tour-and-news/hogans-return-back-tragedy-win-1950-us-open.

Over the course of this campaign we have considered a number of Dream Killers that can steal your future and shipwreck your life plans. Review them and determine which one is the biggest threat to your dreams. Is it the bullying spirit? Is it irresponsible social media, or possibly drug and alcohol temptations? Or maybe it is the way you treat members of the opposite sex. It takes a stand-up person to admit their weaknesses and ask for help. Go to your Power Partner or a coach and seek help in this area. I know this isn't easy, but the things that truly matter rarely are—that's why average people typically don't even try.

TODAY'S ACTION-CHALLENGE

"All of my life I have always had the urge to do things better than anybody else."

"Before I was ever in my teens, I knew exactly what I wanted to be when I grew up. My goal was to be the greatest athlete that ever lived."

—Babe Didrikson Zaharias

Day Thirty-Six

From My Perspective

Raw enthusiasm, God-given talent, passion, competitiveness, and an exuberant spirit. How's that for a résumé? Babe Didrikson Zaharias loved competing, and loved playing the game. What I admire about this legendary athlete is how much fun she had battling at the highest level against the greatest competitors of her era. And she dominated. Do YOU love the game? Are you grateful that you have been chosen to compete and represent your school or organization? Too many athletes have lost their love of the game, and now it's all about personal stats, accolades, and big contracts. What happened to playing the game like we did when we were kids? The truly great ones competed for years at the highest level because they loved it. Find your enthusiasm today, and bring that energy to your whole team. Don't dread practice, relish it, and consider it a gift—because it is. One day you'll tell stories about the things you accomplish today. Maybe others will too.

Fascinating Facts

Babe Didrikson is widely considered one of the greatest athletes of all time. A fierce competitor, Babe won two gold medals in track and field at the 1932 Olympic Games, and went on to win ten LPGA major championships—an amazing feat. In 1953 Didrikson was diagnosed with colon cancer and underwent emergency surgery, and was told she would most likely never play golf again. Babe returned the following year and won the US Women's Open by a record twelve strokes! She was named the Tenth Greatest Athlete of the Twentieth Century by ESPN,[38] and the Ninth Greatest Athlete of the Twentieth Century by the Associated Press.[39] Do you realize there is also greatness hiding inside of you? Uncover it, and unleash it.

Today's Achievements

---

[38] ESPN. "Top N. American athletes of the century." ESPN.com. Accessed September 18, 2017. http://www.espn.com/sportscentury/athletes.html.

[39] Associated Press. *The Sports 100: The 100 Greatest Athletes of the 20th Century.* New York: Associated Press, 1999.

Today I want you to identify, in your opinion, the one player on your team who has demonstrated the most exceptional attitude over the past six weeks, and the one who has been the most positive role model and influencer on your team. Go to that teammate and share with them that you have noticed their example and that you appreciate their leadership. Now strive to imitate their strength of character, and begin to multiply that impact among your entire team. Courage is contagious.

WEEKLY HUDDLE

Week-Six Dream Killer: Alcohol and Drug Abuse

Anxiety and stress among teens today are at all-time highs. The reason? Perceived pressure. The pressure to fit in, make good grades, go to college, get into the right school, drive the right car, wear the right clothes, hang out with the right people, get the right job, and be ACCEPTED. All that pressure is squeezing young people, and the internal struggle can be overwhelming. Add to that social media and the pressure to look cool, and you have yourself the perfect storm. Sadly, many students are turning to drugs and alcohol to ease the pain, not knowing that those choices can lead to extreme danger as a young person, and pain and loss as a future adult. The teenage brain is still forming and developing, and what you put into your body affects that crucial process. How are you treating your decision-making device? All the other Dream Killers are drastically affected by this one treacherous pitfall: bullying and violence, date rape, drunk driving accidents, failing grades, and arrests—all fueled by drug-and-alcohol abuse among young people. And social media gives the dangerous illusion that it's cool. It is not. It's time for you to help change what "cool" looks like among your peers and at your school.

Discussion Questions

1) Talk about a famous athlete who ruined his/her career through drug-and-alcohol abuse. What do you think led to it? How did it progress?

2) Discuss the drug culture at your school. No names, just in general—what are the latest trends?

3) Why do you think Xanax, Oxycontin, and heroin use is skyrocketing among teens today? As an athlete, are you concerned about injuries and opioid addiction?

4) What are three things you can do as a team to turn the tide toward sobriety and a responsible social life among your peers?

Week-Six Power Grade: _____

Three Lessons Learned This Week:

◯

◯

◯

WEEK-SIX POPP EXERCISE
Winning team gets "Hope Is the New Dope" gear!

Time to vote for your POPP superlatives!

- Comeback Player Award
- All Heart Award
- Team Player Award

These standout players will be honored at our 41st Day Celebration. Choose the players who set the best example for the team in attitude, intensity, and effort on and off the field, in the hallways, and in the classrooms.

OVERTIME

I will treat my opponents with dignity and respect, whether we win or lose.

I remember when it was rare to see a player show off or show out after making a big play. When you reach the end zone, act like you've been there before. Today players are taunting and celebrating after they make a seven-yard gain for a first down. Ridiculous. It comes down to respecting the sport, the game, and the competitors. Giving every ounce of your energy and competitive spirit IS respecting the game, but there's no room for taunting or disrespecting your opponent. In fact, it's even more impressive when you knock a guy on his butt, and then help him up (that'll stick in his head more than taunting). There's absolutely nothing wrong with showing your passion as adrenaline blasts, but you actually give some of your power away when you strive to turn the spotlight on yourself—and it also robs the team of its collective energy as you single yourself out.

POPP Power Principle #7
All That I Need, I Already Possess.
Great athletes and standout competitors all possess a rare ability to dig deep into unseen reservoirs and draw out

extra strength when the game is on the line. They seem to be operating by sheer will and instinct, as if all they need is stored up inside and ready when needed. This is why we practice so long and train so hard, so that when the game is on the line we can draw from deep inside, rather than search for external solutions. Again, focus on the things under your control and put in the work behind the scenes so you can dig deep when the spotlight is on you. You have levels of your talent that you have yet to access, and depths of your unique gift that haven't been explored or discovered yet. Practice is where you expand your boundaries and limits, and discover that all you need, you already possess. Find the gift buried deep within you.

Watch Overtime POPP Video

This week we will get into the minds of those who have achieved what few others ever have. **SHOW RESPECT**. Reclaim your power.

CAUTION FLAG

This week SEARCH for positive role models at your schools: down the hallways and in the classrooms. Pay attention—awareness is the first step.

Coaches Corner

Joe Torre[40]

Joe Torre will forever be remembered as a Yankee, but he was an Atlanta Brave first—which is how I tolerated his team in the nineties and early 2000s. If someone had to beat us, it might as well be him. He won with grace and style and never embarrassed his team, family, or fan base by his behavior. His players were loyal to him, and he took responsibility for losses while giving them credit for the victories. He controlled his emotions and made tough decisions under pressure, calmly and confidently. Some opponents make you feel disrespected or "less than" when they beat you, but not Joe. After a loss, your team felt as though they had been bested by someone stronger. And the whole team reflected their manager's demeanor. Can you win with dignity and grace? Can you shake another player's hand at the end of a contest, knowing you did your best, but also acknowledging they did as well? Practice with strong character this week. Win, but win well.

Achievements

Joe Torre managed his New York Yankees to three straight World Series titles in 1998–2000, and won 114 games during the 1998 season. Torre led his teams to the playoffs fourteen times, and he is fourth all time with four World Series titles. Joe also managed the Los Angeles Dodgers from 2008 to 2010, winning two more division titles.

---

[40] "Joe Torre," Baseball Hall of Fame website, accessed August 22, 2017, http://baseballhall.org/hof/torre-joe.

Joe Torre coached with class, calm, and an unflappable demeanor, and he won a lot of games along the way, always being one of those managers players wanted to play for. Do your teammates love to follow you?

"Competing at the highest level is not about winning. It's about preparation, courage, understanding and nurturing your people, and heart. Winning is the result."

"Respect is the word I want. You have to earn it. You give, and you get it in return. That's how I see it."

—Joe Torre

PEYTON MANNING

"My closest friends are from my high school days."

"Pressure is something you feel when you don't know what the hell you're doing."

—Peyton Manning

Day Thirty-Seven

From My Perspective

Peyton Manning was another player I loved to hate when he played against my Georgia Bulldogs. However, he was also someone who made hating him almost impossible because of his extraordinary character. He rarely took the credit, accepted the praise, or boasted of his achievements. Instead, he let his game do the talking. Playing quarterback for the Colts and the Broncos, it was like his team had another offensive coordinator under center. After so many hours studying game films and playbooks before and after regular practice times, he came to understand the game so well that he became one of the most effective on-field game managers the NFL has ever seen. How hard are you willing to work to fully understand your coach's game plan? The mental game is just as important, even more so, than physical ability alone. Put in the work and master the system entrusted to you.

Fascinating Facts

Peyton Manning is a fourteen-time Pro-Bowler, a five-time League MVP, a two-time Super Bowl Champion, and 2012 Come Back Player of the Year. Manning is part of football's Royal Family: his father, Archie Manning played sixteen seasons in the NFL, and was inducted into the College Football Hall of Fame; and his brother Eli is a two-time Super Bowl Champion quarterback with the New York Giants. Peyton is a student and a professor of the game. It is said that within a week after he was drafted by Indianapolis, he had memorized the Colts' playbook, and he is currently able to remember the details and timing of specific plays from his days all the way back at the University of Tennessee.[41] Are you willing to invest in yourself and in your dreams? Put in the work.

Today's Achievements

[41] Schwab, Frank. May 2, 2013. "Peyton Manning recalls every detail of play at Tennessee in 1996, and it is simply amazing." Yahoo Sports. Accessed September 18, 2017. https://sports.yahoo.com/blogs/ncaaf-dr-saturday/peyton-manning-recalls-every-detail-play-tennessee-1996-140742956.html.

Today I want you to be a servant. Show up early and see how you can help. Ask your coaches or trainer what you can do to assist. The more important your role on your team, the bigger the impact when you SERVE. Can you help set up for drills? Can you lead the team in a devotional? Can you stay after and help clean up? Be a sacrificial servant today and let everyone see your heart to pitch in and help. Others will see your example and follow suit, and your coaches will see a difference too.

ALTHEA GIBSON

"I always wanted to be somebody. If I made it, it's half because I was game enough to take a lot of punishment along the way and half because there were a lot of people who cared enough to help me."

"Shaking hands with the Queen of England was a long way from being forced to sit in the colored section of the bus going into downtown Wilmington, North Carolina."

—Althea Gibson

Day Thirty-Eight

From My Perspective

I am so honored to highlight these amazing, beautiful brothers and sisters who played their respective sports under tremendous pressure during an ugly time in our nation's history. Althea Gibson crossed the color line during a time when Dr. King was emerging as the leader of the American civil rights movement. I played college athletics and I remember the pressure to make the team, be a starter, and then win my starting position back after I lost it—and be a student athlete at the same time. But the pressure I felt was merely time management, discipline, and focus. I cannot fathom trying to play my sport while being hated, threatened, and tormented, while still expected to be the best. That takes a truly extraordinary individual, which Ms. Gibson was. Can you rise above and stay focused when you face ridicule, opposition, rumors, or school drama? It takes a bigger person to walk away sometimes, than to fight against things that don't deserve your time or attention. Stand for the truth, and be a role model in your community. Lord knows we need some.

Fascinating Facts

Althea Gibson was an outstanding professional tennis player and golfer, but it was her tremendous impact on sports beyond the court that earned her a place in history.

She was born to parents who worked as sharecroppers on a cotton farm. Because of the Great Depression, Althea's family moved to Harlem. Althea broke the color barrier in her sport right at the beginning of the civil rights movement, which took tremendous courage. She was the first person of color to win a Grand Slam title, and she went on to win ten more during her brilliant career. She also became the first black player to compete on the women's pro golf tour.[42] Ms. Gibson has often been compared to Jackie Robinson, and I for one second that notion.

Today's Achievements

---

[42] Alvarez, Anya. February 20, 2017. "The lesser-known history of Althea Gibson the golfer." ESPNW. Accessed September 18, 2017. http://www.espn.com/espnw/culture/article/18724493/the-lesser-known-history-althea-gibson-golfer.

We've almost reached the finish line in this forty-day journey. Your coaches and trainers have guided you through this process together. Now I want you to take initiative along with your other team leaders. If your coaches agree, call a "players-only" meeting with the other POPP40 participants. Have an honest discussion about why you are doing this and what you hope to accomplish. This should be a serious talk to see if everyone is now on the same page. Remind one another what you have committed to and what you are striving to accomplish as a team, and WHY. This will help you identify who the leaders really are and get everyone of one heart and one mind. It doesn't need to be long, but make it powerful.

PETE MARAVICH

"There is nothing wrong with dedication and goals, but if you focus on yourself, all the lights fade away and you become a fleeting moment in life."

"I got by on talent. That was my fatal mistake."

—Pete Maravich

226

Day Thirty-Nine

From My Perspective

In the seventies as a kid, Pete Maravich was my favorite player, and there wasn't a close second. I was so excited when he signed with my Atlanta Hawks and got the richest contract in NBA history at that time. He revolutionized the game and did things with ball no one had even imagined. He averaged an unbelievable forty-four points a game during his career at LSU.[43] Many called him a "Showboat," but crowds still came to watch the spectacle: ball handling, no-look passes, and dizzying moves that left defenders confused and off balance. I also loved his superstition: his signature old, worn-out socks he wore over his game socks in every game; the same socks, year after year, game after game. He loved the game, and he loved pleasing the crowds and giving them their money's worth. Are you aware that the "crowds" are watching you too? Many of them will follow your example and imitate your behavior. All of us are role models. Either we're a good example, or a bad one; you get to choose which. Be a healthy role model today for your followers. It matters more than you know.

---

[43] Myron Medcalf, "What If 'Pistol' Pete Had a 3-Point Line?" *ESPN* The Magazine, August 18, 2014, http://www.espn.com/blog/collegebasketballnation/post/_/id/99934/what-if-pistol-pete-had-a-3-point-line.

Fascinating Facts

Pete Maravich was a five-time NBA All Star, 1977 NBA Scoring Champion, and NCAA Division One All-Time Scoring Champion. Maravich played in the NBA for ten years, and then after his retirement, at the age of forty, he died of a heart attack while playing basketball. Ironically, at the age of twenty-six, at the peak of his career, Pete told the *Beaver County Times*, "I don't want to play ten years in the NBA and then die of a heart attack at the age of forty."[44] That's exactly what he did. Live life fully today; it's all we have.

Today's Achievements

---

[44] Associated Press, "Maravich Said in 1974: 'I Don't Want . . . to Die of a Heart Attack at Age 40," *Los Angeles Times*, January 7, 1988, http://articles.latimes.com/1988-01-07/sports/sp-34024_1_fan-reaction-read-beaver-county-times.

It's time to look back and evaluate your progress. If you have given your all to this program, then you have seen some dramatic results. Now go back and review the goals you wrote down at the beginning of this project. Identify the areas where you have made the most improvement, and acknowledge your victory. But also determine the areas that still need the most attention, and resolve to never give up. Maybe your goals were centered around weight, speed, technique, or size. Maybe they were character goals around overcoming destructive habits or unhealthy patterns. If they were overall team goals, then look and see if you've noticed progress in those areas collectively. Either way, it is time to reassess and focus on consistent growth. Grade yourself today on your overall effort and commitment. Be honest: A or B? C? Hopefully nobody failed, for you were chosen as leaders. Recommit and continue to improve. This is only the beginning.

"Our responsibility in life is not to lie around and wait for things to happen. Our responsibility in life is to work. Life is getting out and getting things done."

"I was a fat little kid with a speech impediment. I used to get beat up, not just picked on."

—Herschel Walker

Day Forty

From My Perspective

I was a student at the University of Georgia when I saw Herschel Walker play for the first time. Eighty thousand fans would shout his name, one side of the stadium shouting "HERSCHEL" and the other side answering "WALKER" over and over. It was electrifying, and I've never seen anything like it since. Herschel's size, speed, and agility were something the NCAA had never witnessed before. And the amazing thing was that he rarely, if ever, had trained in the gym or with weights growing up. He simply ran, stretched, and did a staggering number of push-ups, pull-ups, and sit-ups in his spare time every day—for years. The thing I most admire about Herschel is his humility. I met him in an airport one time and he was so gentle, soft spoken, and warmhearted. All he talked about was helping kids, which is my passion. Of all the touchdowns he scored, and there were so many, never once did he celebrate and bring attention or glory to himself. He simply handed the ball to the referee and trotted back to the sideline. Could you do that? If the crowds shouted your name, could you stay humble? If you can master that, you can change the world. Do your best today, and don't worry about who gets the credit.

Fascinating Facts

Herschel Walker's passion, discipline, and intensity are legendary. It is said that his DAILY routine in junior high included 1,500 push-ups and 2,500 sit-ups. Overweight as a child and plagued by a stuttering problem, Herschel had to work harder than the rest. He read aloud to himself until he overcame his speech impediment, and because of his incredible workout regimen, he became an athletic superstar. He even graduated valedictorian of his graduating class. He credited his mother for teaching him, "If you're going to do anything, do it well. Do it as if Jesus were watching you."[45] He most certainly did.

Today's Achievements

---

[45] "Herschel Walker's Battle with D.I.D.," Christian Broadcasting Network, accessed August 22, 2017, http://www1.cbn.com/700club/herschel-walkers-battle-did.

Choose one of your teammates who you would vote as the "Most Improved Player" over these past forty days. This would be the player who demonstrated the most radical change of mind and heart as a result of these daily challenges. (Write their name down in your journal.) Now choose the player who you think is the "Most Valuable Player" overall, who displayed the strongest leadership skills and was the most positive role model to the coaches and rest of the team. These will be tallied and standout players will be acknowledged and rewarded at our 41st Day Celebration.

WEEKLY HUDDLE

Overtime Dream Killer:
Lowering Scholastic Standards

I know sometimes you must wonder why you have to study, learn, and be tested on things you can't imagine using later in life. I know I did. But now I know what I didn't know then: grades reveal character. It's not just the information you are learning, but more importantly the discipline and work ethic it takes to excel and thrive in that area of your life. It all goes together. However, there is a new mentality growing in today's student culture: being smart is not seen as cool anymore. That couldn't be farther from the truth. The student athlete is the ultimate role model at your age. You are destined to be a success, whatever that looks like for you, if you can handle the pressure and stress of sports AND scholastics at a high level. When you graduate, you will be in great demand, because you will be a young person of character. Whatever you do, do not be a distraction in the classroom; do not disrespect your teachers by not giving them your full attention; don't use your phone in class; don't settle for less than your best just because you're an athlete—the opposite should be true. Unfortunately, once again, athletes are oftentimes the students who are lowering the standards for excellence for the entire school, because others are following their lead. Doing your best in the classroom IS cool. Convince others to follow your example.

Discussion Questions

1) Do you consider yourself a role model in academics? Explain why or why not. Talk about a non-sports-related dream you have for your life.

2) Describe yourself ten years from today (where you live, what you do for a living, are you married, etc.). The more details, the better.

3) Discuss the growing mentality among students that it isn't "cool" to be smart. Where do you think that came from, and why is it spreading?

4) What are three things you can do as a team to raise the overall standards for scholastic achievement at your school?

Overtime Power Grade: _____

Three Lessons Learned This Week:

○

○

○

OVERTIME POPP EXERCISE
Winning team gets "Hope Is the New Dope" gear!

WANT TO GET STRONGER?

PRACTICE LIFTING OTHERS.

Participate in our life-changing 40 Days of Power program and get to work changing some lives of your own.

PowerOfPeaceProject.com

Each One Lift One

- Choose a new training partner who has not gone through this program. Teach them the principles you have learned from this project, and bring them into the **POPP SQUAD.**

- Create your POPP CLUB social-media group, so that others at your school can follow your lead. It's all about momentum— keep the Protect the Dream Campaign moving!

- As a team, choose another school in your region that you would like to sponsor and pass this project along to. Let's start a teen movement that rolls from one athlete to the next, from one school to another, and all across the state. Let's **Protect the Dreams** of a young generation on the verge of changing the world. You ARE the SOLUTION.

Day Forty-One Bonus

From My Perspective

Roger Bannister was the first to break the four-minute mile. For decades, it seemed to many an impossible barrier to break through. He accomplished the feat on May 6, 1954, running a time of 3 minutes 59.4 seconds. After all those years, the seemingly impossible was achieved, but surprisingly, the record lasted only forty-six days. Over the next five years, another five seconds had been shaved off.[46] You see, the barrier was purely man-made and nothing but a thin glass ceiling. Once someone had proven that it could be done, then others began to do it as well. What are your limits? Are they nothing more than conditioned thinking you have acquired by comparing yourself to others? No one can tell you what you are capable of but you. Break through your limitations in the same way you break through that paper banner when you burst onto the field. Everything is impossible until someone does it.

Day Forty-One POPP Challenge

The meaning of life is to find your gift; the purpose of life is to give it to the world. No one has ever been given your exact gift in the style and measure in which you were

---

[46] Joel Runyon, "Impossible Case Study: Sir Roger Bannister and the Four-Minute Mile," Impossible X, April 5, 2014, https://impossiblehq.com/impossible-case-study-sir-roger-bannister/.

given it. What is your ONE thing, that thing that makes you "come alive" when you do it? It lies hidden within and must be uncovered. Do you truly love the game you have been blessed to play since you were little boys and little girls? Sports teach us life lessons that we can seldom learn anywhere else. I would be a whole different human being today if I had not been an athlete. Not better or worse, just different.

Do this one thing for me: be the best you can be. There's never been another you, and there never will be. Don't settle. Don't get satisfied. Stay hungry, and run. Yeah, run fast. Hustle. Never, ever, ever give up. Ever. You were born to be great. Find your greatness within, and then go find what makes you come ALIVE. Now more than ever, the world needs young people who have come alive. Ride that one thing till the wheels fall off. You got this—now go get yours.

Today's Achievements

Closing

Congratulations! You have worked hard and pushed yourself in areas that many athletes neglect. Over the past forty days, you have looked into the lives of men and women who achieved extraordinary feats and accomplishments, and in some cases, changed their world. You have broken unhealthy habits and created new, healthy patterns that provide you with unlimited power and potential. You have meditated on quotes, completed action-challenges, worked in small groups, and strived to accomplish challenging goals that expanded your limits beyond where they were just forty short days ago. You have completed something significant and forged stronger character. Well done, we are proud of you. But where will you go from here?

This campaign is built for athletes and student leaders. You have been blessed with gifts, abilities, and talents that many other students do not possess. Because of these, you have been afforded certain privileges that come along with those gifts. You are typically a part of the "in" group and have a certain level of popularity, which feels good. However, these gifts are not yours, but rather given to you by your Creator, and given so that you would share them with the world. The meaning of life is to discover your unique gift; the purpose of life is to give that gift to those who need it. The challenge going forward is to continue your progress and become the role models your school desperately needs. Imagine the impact you could have if the whole team came together behind these principles, and shifted your school culture toward compassion and acceptance. You have the influence, you have the voice, you have the juice. Now, choose to use your collective and individual influence and newfound power for PEACE. I promise you will have no regrets if you walk in these ways, and believe it or not, you will even save some lives along the way. There is no greater impact than that.

You can be heroes, and it starts today. Let's get busy, and may God bless you along your unique journey.

Now Let's Celebrate Our New POPP SQUADS!

Now for the 41st Day Celebration! It's time to recognize and honor your victories over the last forty days. POPP Certificates of Achievement will be given, as well as special awards to the standout players from this project. The Best Overall Team Award will be presented to the winning team's coach. We will enjoy motivational and entertaining presentations by rival POPP Squads, and musical guests and celebrity speakers will inspire us. The night will end with our very special Mason Tompkins Legacy Award.

Coach Matt Dickmann presenting POPP's biggest award

The Mason Tompkins Legacy Award is given to the player who most exemplifies the positive, young role model, and most embodies the character, attitude, and courage of the **Protect the Dream** Team. It was named after a young man at Harrison High School whom we lost too young. He was a standout athlete and an even better human being. Read the words of Wade Tompkins, Mason's dad, below:

"My family and I are extremely honored that you have named the award given to the standout athlete that most exemplifies the Seven Steps to Power and the core ideals of

Protect the Dream, the 'Mason Tompkins Legacy Award'. Mason was a young man whom teachers and coaches wanted in their classroom and on the field. He went out of his way to make everyone smile. Even at an early age he modeled the Seven Steps in his life.

"The naming of this award and including Mason in your program will allow his memory to carry on. He will be able to continue to help and inspire others, which is what he did and always wanted to do. His ultimate goal was to work in a profession that would allow him to do just that.

"As a parent and coach, you always are trying to teach and guide in order to lead your child or player down a life-fulfilling path. In reading this book and the Seven Steps to Power, if I could write what I believe, and tried to teach, this would be it. I thank you as a parent and a coach for conveying

Mason Tompkins

244

these messages to empower today's youth, and for allowing my family to be part of it."

Cameron Messina (right) from Harrison High School, our first Mason Tompkins Legacy Award winner. Pictured with Mason's father, Wade Tompkins (left), and POPP founder Kit Cummings (center).

"There will be tough times in your life, but it's how you come through those tough times that makes you stronger than you were before. Always remember that God has a plan for your life, and I promise that the tough times will be more than worth it."

—Cameron Messina

This quote was written the week after Cameron tore the ACL in his right knee in the first game of his senior season—less than one year after he had torn the ACL in his left knee halfway through his junior year. He had just won the Legacy Award the week prior to his injury. His exceptional attitude is what makes Cameron a team leader on the field, in the hallways, and in his community. Cameron exemplifies the warrior spirit, and the character and courage that the POPP Legacy Award is given for. He was a good friend of Mason's and competed with and against him for years. Cameron won't be the last, but he will always be the first player to win the Mason Tompkins Legacy Award.

On the award these words are engraved:

> *"The gold standard student athlete possessing a genuine spirit, heart, and work ethic that impacts people on and off the field. The type of friend we all want. A role-model that all young men and women should strive to become in all areas of life."*

Now, let's charge out of the tunnel together. Let's use our considerable influence and change what "cool" looks like in our schools and communities. There's no competition when it comes to saving young lives, so let's all work together. You are now the role models, pacesetters, and Ambassadors for Peace on your team and in your school. We are all proud of your achievement. Now keep the momentum going, and I'll see you on the field.

A Final Word

You have spent the past eight weeks training yourself to be the best you can be as an athlete and a leader. Now is the time to show those around you what you have been working on. One of the most famous stories in all of scripture is the one about the undersized kid named David and the daunting giant named Goliath. For forty days, the army of Israel ran back from the battle line against this giant and cowered in their corner. Then David, this shepherd boy, showed up to the battle, and with a sling and some stones, squared the giant up and killed him. It was an epic event that changed the whole course of a nation.

However, the greatest line is tucked away in the story when scripture says:

> *"When the Philistines saw that their hero was dead, they turned and ran. Then the men of Israel and Judah surged forward with a shout and pursued the Philistines"* (1 Sam. 17:51–52, NIV).

The boldness of ONE affected an entire army! I love the phrase "they surged ahead." That, my friend, is called momentum.

You are set and ready to go. Now be bold and chase down some giants! I promise you this, when you do, the team around you will surge forward and feed off the momentum you helped create! **Protect the Dream**.

Mike Linch, Senior Pastor
NorthStar Church, Kennesaw, GA

POPP founder Kit Cummings with Allatoona and Alexander POPP squads after a hard-fought battle

About the Author

Kit Cummings is an international speaker, teacher, and award-winning author with the gift to evoke goose bumps, laughter, and even tears in his audiences. Whether he is speaking to large corporations, small businesses, sports teams, churches, schools, or even the toughest prisons in America, Kit spreads his message of power, potential, and positive change through his seminars and keynotes. Kit has spoken to tens of thousands of people all over the world.

Born and raised in Atlanta, Kit earned a BBA in marketing from the Terry School of Business at the University of Georgia, and he also holds a master of theology. Kit founded the Power of Peace Project, and brings his experience working in some of the most dangerous areas in the world into schools and corporations to bring about community change. Kit has negotiated peace between some of the most notorious gangs in America's underculture, and has spoken at the Gandhi Global Peace Summit in Durban, South Africa. Kit has authored six books and hosts Power of Peace Radio.

Book Kit for your next event!

KitCummings.com
PowerofPeaceProject.com
Facebook/KitCummings
@PowerofPeace88
Instagram/KitCummings88
LinkedIn/Kit Cummings